Vital Behavior Blueprint

5 Steps to Embed Mission-Critical Habits into Your Organization's DNA

JULIE M. SMITH, PHD
LORI LUDWIG, PHD

© 2024 by Performance Ally

All rights reserved, including the right of reproduction in whole or in part in any form.

ISBN: 979-8-9889461-3-7 (print)
ISBN: 979-8-9889461-0-6 (ebook)

First Printing: 2024

The following terms are trademarks of Performance Ally:

- Ally Assist™
- Ally Feedback Loops™
- Ally Network™
- Behavior-Powered Results™
- Organizational Behavior Momentum™
- Perfect Care Visit™
- Performance Ally™
- Vital Behavior Blueprint™

Dedication

I dedicate this book to Dr. Leslie Braksick, my fearless partner in co-founding CLG (ALULA), and fellow Big Wave Surfer in Organizational Behavior Management. Your unique blend of optimism and practicality taught our clients worldwide that there's no challenge too great if we tackle it with the help of Behavior Science. You've changed their lives, and you changed mine the day we met.

—Julie M. Smith

I dedicate this work to Dr. Tim Ludwig. You are an inspiration to me and countless others to keep advancing the science of Organizational Behavior Management.

—Lori Ludwig

Contents

Our Discovery of the Science and Art of Vital Behaviors

1

THE BASICS
How Vital Behaviors Become Organizational Habits
11

1. Why Vital Behaviors Produce Remarkable Results 13
2. How to Find Vital Behaviors in Your Organization 25
3. The 3 Pillars to Transform Vital Behaviors into Sustainable Habits 37
4. Move Beyond Top-Down Management to Build Engaged Ally Networks 51
5. Quick Start Guide to the 5 Steps for Building a Vital Behavior Blueprint 59

BUILD A VITAL BEHAVIOR BLUEPRINT IN 5 STEPS
How to Embed Mission-Critical Habits into Your Organization's DNA
67

6. Step 1: Prioritize Behavior-Powered Results 73
7. Step 2: Identify Key Performer Groups 85
8. Step 3: Clarify Vital Behaviors 93
9. Step 4: "Wire" Ally Networks 105
10. Step 5: Build Habits Using 3 Pillars 115

VITAL BEHAVIOR SUCCESS STORIES
Tales from the Trenches
127

11. In-Home Repair Techs Grow Their Business by Respecting Customers in a Whole New Way 129
12. A Nursing Home Rehabilitates Its Reputation from "Stay Away!" to "The Place to Stay!" 149

BEYOND BASICS
Demystifying the Science and Art Behind Our Success
171

13. Behavior Analysis: The Science of *Individual* Behavior Change 173
14. Organizational Behavior Management (OBM): Behavior Analysis Applied in Organizations 181
15. The Art of Navigating Emotions and Changing Mindsets 189

In Conclusion, One More Promise to You . . .
205

MORE . . .
209

Want More Tools? 211
Want to Learn More About Organizational Behavior Management (OBM)? 213
Acknowledgments 215
About the Authors 219
About Performance Ally 221
Notes 223

Our Discovery of the Science and Art of Vital Behaviors

Julie's Story

In 2013, my perfect life began to unravel. It happened during a board meeting at an academic health system. When I mentioned my husband's upcoming brain surgery at our flagship hospital, a look of profound concern swept across a fellow board member's face as she shook her head slowly. Her reaction worried me. After all, she was a seasoned medical professional, and I was not.

I waited until a break to ask her, "Why not here? They seem well-equipped." She met my gaze directly, lowered her voice, and shared a stark revelation, "That surgery is highly risky. Only a few surgeons in the country can handle it safely." She directed us to one of the world's premiere healthcare systems where we discovered the original diagnosis was incorrect—my husband needed his thyroid removed, not brain surgery. However, complications arose after what appeared to be routine surgery, and he suffered brain damage due to oxygen deprivation.

Around this time, my son, who suffered from severe migraines, decided to pause his education to seek medical attention. I was too consumed with my husband's recovery to attend his care visits. Tragically, a few months after starting a new medication, my son passed away suddenly.

Besides the overwhelming grief, guilt consumed me. I felt I could have done more to prevent these tragedies. After all, I was an organizational behavior consultant. The consulting company I co-founded had won global awards for bringing about large-scale behavior change. We had a long track record of helping top-tier clients execute strategic initiatives and improve performance. Why hadn't I intervened here? I tossed and turned at night, replaying events in my head. Were there things our family should have done differently? Or our care teams?

My breaking point came when I met with hospital personnel to reconstruct events. It became evident that both my husband's and son's medical complications resulted from human errors. My son's death was due to a medication error, arising from a lack of communication between physicians. In my husband's case, two doctors had become fixated on the novel brain surgery and missed the massive nodules on his thyroid, escalating the risks involved in his thyroidectomy.

My grief and guilt turned into seething anger. I was furious with myself for having blindly trusted the healthcare system, and incensed at the physicians and their leaders for allowing unsafe practices to persist. I felt frozen for months, torn between pursuing legal action, improving healthcare delivery, or simply walking away.

What turned it around for me was when the CEO and Chief Nursing Officer of the flagship hospital invited me to help create an error-free hospital, leveraging my expertise as a behavior-change consultant. Having open access to the hospital, I soon discovered that healthcare teams were genuinely trying to improve but lacked the critical knowledge to help each other establish good habits. When I attempted to introduce the behavior-based techniques we had developed at my company, the teams found it too complex to execute.

I realized that our approach needed to be simplified to match the fast-paced healthcare environment. It had to be easily understood and applied by everyone, from housekeepers to physicians. More importantly, it needed to be embraced by grassroots employees and their leaders, rather than imposed by executives and consultants.

Following this realization, I made the decision to leave the company I had co-founded 20 years earlier and concentrate on developing a simplified method to instill mission-critical habits at scale within healthcare. At that point, I knew that healthcare professionals typically adhered to best practices less than 40% of the time. My goal was to increase adherence to 90% or better. Achieving this goal would not only transform healthcare but also benefit every other industry.

However, it proved to be a daunting task to simplify the complex organizational behavior change models my colleagues and I had developed with our clients over decades. Every word and tool seemed indispensable, making it challenging to consolidate or eliminate them. After a few years of incremental progress testing simpler models on real healthcare projects, I realized I needed help from a seasoned behavioral colleague who had traveled a similar path as a consultant.

It was then that Lori Ludwig reached out to collaborate with me, as if by fate. We discovered that we were both on similar journeys, aiming to make it easy for organizations to integrate essential habits into their DNA.

Lori's Story

I spent years working in the corporate and non-profit worlds, specializing in designing the behavior-change component of large-scale performance-improvement initiatives. My role involved collaborating with internal change agents such as Learning and Development executives, Lean Six Sigma teams, boards, special committees, and Human Resources to design groundbreaking initiatives that would stick. But, despite the initial splash, the new programs and practices we developed often faded. Leaders failed to reinforce the necessary behavior changes, and my frustration grew.

My performance consulting work within global corporations, small businesses, and non-profits all revealed a harsh truth: Clients craved quick, effortless solutions, not comprehensive behavioral systems to manage. So whenever I struggled or hit a brick wall, I clung to the mantra, "Make it as simple as possible."

My breaking point arrived during a strategy meeting with a client. Despite my best efforts to synthesize a complex change effort into a simplified action plan, the executive in charge rejected it in front of everyone! Maybe it was the visibility I brought to the disconnects in their systems and how much work she'd need to do, or the latest article she read about a quick solution. I walked out of that meeting and thought, "I'm tired of trying to build lasting systems; it's impossible. I'm done!"

Then, in this "I'm done" phase, I was invited to an international conference to speak about how behavioral systems could solve big problems. I knew this would be a challenge for me, given that I was about to give up on this work, so I played it safe and focused my talk on performance-based training. People got that, even with translation issues. I was relieved.

But the turning point for me that happened at this conference was when I saw Julie speak. When she shared her vision for solving problems in healthcare systems, it reignited my enthusiasm. Her different approach to large-scale behavior change fascinated me. It seemed faster, simpler—and produced lasting results. Eager to learn more, I reached out, offering help. To my surprise, Julie welcomed collaboration. For the last several years, we've teamed up to distill the complexity of our science into practical tools that any organization can implement. The lesson I've learned through all this is how important collaboration is with those who share a similar vision. Julie has helped me see behavior change through a different lens, and as Dr. Wayne Dyer said, "When you change the way you look at things, the things you look at change."

How We Learned to Embed Organizational Habits

We both were in college when we learned about Behavior Analysis, the science of what works in behavior change. We fell in love with the science because it offered a new world view of why people do what they do. Rather than blaming people for their poor habits, Behavior Analysis focuses on altering the environment to help them succeed.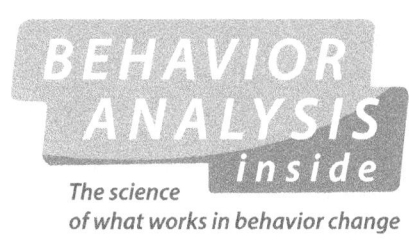

The science of what works in behavior change

We found it to be a very positive, practical approach. We saw that the principles and methods empowered individuals to improve a variety of behaviors, from helping students excel at school to assisting people in becoming healthier, wealthier, and better versions of themselves.

At the time, Organizational Behavior Management (OBM), a subspecialty of Behavior Analysis, was just starting to get traction. It focuses on pinpointing mission-critical behaviors and changing work environments to help employees do those behaviors to improve business results. We call these behaviors Vital Behaviors.

Vital Behaviors

The vital few mission-critical behaviors that will dramatically improve targeted results when a large group of people make them habits.

As we all know, many behaviors contribute to the achievement of business results. But Vital Behaviors follow the 80/20 rule: 80% of an organization's results stem from just 20% of the key repetitive actions taken by its employees. When these Vital Behaviors are executed correctly and consistently by many, the organization's results soar.

We both learned how to find Vital Behaviors and implement OBM by working on projects in our respective university towns: One was at a local print shop and the other with an international nonprofit association. We quickly found that most employees and volunteers (1) lacked clear expectations about what they should do, (2) got very little feedback—or worse, only got feedback when something went wrong—and (3) experienced many barriers to doing the right things.

For example, at the print shop, a Vital Behavior was to "fill out the print job order forms correctly." However, unclear instructions often led to mistakes, customer dissatisfaction, and costly rework, causing the owner to become upset with employees. Because employees felt they could never do anything right, turnover became a big problem, making it difficult to have trained staff ready to do quality work. This vicious cycle repeated itself every day. No one was happy.

To break this cycle, managers were trained to clarify expectations for all staff regarding form accuracy and to focus on "catching people doing things right." The back-end staff was tasked with monitoring form accuracy for orders processed by the front-counter staff. Each morning, team members met to review data from the prior day: The percentage of order forms completed correctly (the Vital Behavior) compared to the percentage of orders accepted by customers without the need for rework (the desired outcome). Whenever obstacles emerged, employees were empowered to swiftly address and eliminate them.

Implementing these changes took just two weeks, but the impact was profound. Employees and managers became energized by working toward shared goals and witnessing tangible progress. Results improved significantly and remained consistent over time, and the turnover problem vanished entirely.

Heady from our early successes, over the next few decades we both went on to conduct larger and larger projects, from individual work units to global engagements with some of the world's largest companies. It was exhilarating to be part of helping our clients achieve amazing results through targeted change of Vital Behaviors across hundreds and even thousands of people. With our clients, we showcased these results in conference presentations, books, articles, and dozens of case studies. Our clients were recognized for being best-in-class for process improvement, sales, operational excellence, forecast accuracy, return-on-capital-employed, customer service, and much more—all due to the fact that these efforts were Vital Behavior–powered.

The Science and Art of Vital Behaviors

We wish we could say it was easy, but it wasn't. In fact, Julie named her first consulting company the Continuous Learning Group (CLG) for a reason—because she and her colleagues were constantly challenged to learn new things in order to apply the science of individual behavior change on such an unprecedented scale. What we both learned is that embedding Vital Behaviors into an organization's DNA is both a science and an art. Let's break it down.

The science of identifying and embedding Vital Behaviors organizationally. Science involves using data and research-backed methods to pinpoint and rigorously test the behaviors that are most crucial for achieving desired outcomes. This may entail analyzing past performance data, watching people implement work processes to see where missteps regularly occur, studying industry best practices, and conducting experiments to validate Vital Behaviors.

A scientific approach also requires creating systems and processes that support and reinforce these behaviors consistently over time. This includes fostering a culture where these behaviors are not only encouraged but also celebrated.

The art of changing mindsets and emotions. The art of behavior change involves helping individuals navigate the emotions and beliefs that inevitably arise when changing habits. This includes assessing an individual's readiness for change and meeting them where they are—whether they are resistant, receptive, or resilient. Each reaction to change is valid to that person. By adjusting your approach to fit the person's current state, you can help them see the benefits of adopting the Vital Behaviors, so they ultimately are doing things they feel good about and believe in.

Overall, the process of embedding Vital Behaviors is a dynamic and ongoing effort that requires a combination of scientific rigor and creative problem-solving. It's about finding the right balance between data-driven insights and human-centered approaches to create lasting change within the organization.

Why We Wrote This Book

Our goal is to help organizations form mission-critical habits with ease, without a lot of expensive hand-holding! When it comes to behavior change at scale, we want readers to feel confident enough to do it themselves.

We've dedicated years to developing the Vital Behavior Blueprint, a practical guide with 5 Steps for embedding mission-critical habits into an organization's DNA. Through continuous testing with innovative leaders from diverse organizations, these steps consistently proved their effectiveness. What would typically take weeks or months to achieve was accomplished in just days with our streamlined 5-Step Blueprint. Witnessing this unprecedented efficiency in driving widespread behavior change, we are excited to share this impactful methodology with you.

What's Next in Your Vital Behavior Journey?

In this book we take you on a journey divided into four parts:

The Basics: How Vital Behaviors Become Organizational Habits. Chapters 1–5 reveal why Vital Behaviors produce such remarkable results, and offer insights into identifying them for your organization. You'll learn about the 3 Pillars every employee needs to solidify Vital Behaviors into durable habits: (1) Clear Expectations, (2) Actionable Feedback, and (3) Barrier Removal. You'll also learn how to advance from traditional top-down management to a powerful network of engaged employees who use the 3 Pillars to form new habits together. Finally, you will be provided with a Quick Start Guide outlining the 5 Steps for crafting a Vital Behavior Blueprint. This guide will come to life through a brief story about how an executive team implemented Vital Behaviors for themselves to gain significant momentum on a global strategic initiative.

Build a Vital Behavior Blueprint in 5 Steps: How to Embed Mission-Critical Habits into Your Organization's DNA. Chapters 6–10 show you exactly how to build your own Vital Behavior Blueprint. Learn along with "Darlene," a hospice agency owner, how to pull together a Vital Behavior Blueprint that improves multiple outcomes.

Vital Behavior Success Stories: Tales from the Trenches. In Chapters 11–12, you'll read stories from organizations that successfully used the Vital Behavior Blueprint to achieve unprecedented results. Our promise: You will gain many ideas to use immediately in your organization.

Beyond the Basics: Demystifying the Science and Art Behind Our Success. Chapters 13–15 reveal the underlying science and art behind changing not only behaviors, but also emotions and mindsets. You'll learn how to create an environment that ensures people are doing Vital Behaviors they feel good about and believe in.

How You Will Benefit from This Book

The Vital Behavior Blueprint is a new, practical guide for turning best practices into standard practices—or habits—for a work unit, site, organization, or even for the clients your organization serves. Often, leaders at all levels find this hard to accomplish. It's difficult to get even the simplest behaviors to become consistent habits. We promise you three benefits. You will:

1. Gain an understanding of what Vital Behaviors are and why they are essential to developing the habits that ensure your organization's success.

2. Discover the Vital Behavior Blueprint, a groundbreaking 5-Step method for aligning and motivating people at scale to consistently execute those Vital Behaviors, and update them as new challenges arise.

3. Build habits in a way that makes your people feel appreciated every day for doing the right things.

In this book we are sharing our core tools developed over decades of successful global consulting. Why? Because it's time to make behavior change at scale easy. Our mission is to enable people and organizations to improve anything through smart, supportive, collective action. Our approach means less stress, better results, and greater job satisfaction. With a Vital Behavior Blueprint, everything works better. We can't wait to hear about your success!

Want more tools?
Access our **HUB** on page 211 to get free *Vital Behavior Blueprint Templates* and more.

THE BASICS

How Vital Behaviors Become Organizational Habits

In this section, we provide essential insights to help you understand the concept of Vital Behaviors and how to transform them into organizational habits. Through numerous short stories, you'll discover that mobilizing people's behavior is a practical and cost-effective method to execute organizational initiatives and plans.

1

Why Vital Behaviors Produce Remarkable Results

Here's a quick quiz so you can evaluate how good your organization is at execution. It's important, because it will tell you if this book will help you. (We are betting it will!)

QUICK QUIZ
Does Your Organization Execute Consistently*?

Our People . . .	Consistently	Inconsistently**
Deliver a great customer experience.	☐	☐
Follow quality and safety protocols.	☐	☐
Implement and sustain new strategic initiatives, process improvements, or best practices.	☐	☐
Achieve project goals and business plans.	☐	☐
Create behavior change in the populations our organization serves.	☐	☐

* Consistently = we do this correctly each and every time (no variation).
** Inconsistently = we have unwanted and unproductive variability.

If you answered "Inconsistently" to any of these questions, we wrote this book for you. And you are not alone. It's been estimated that over 50% of needed performance-improvement efforts fail or take forever to get embedded in organizations. One healthcare provider blew our minds when she shared, "Did you know it takes 17 years on average to get new, life-saving procedures to be adopted universally in a hospital?"

Poor execution doesn't have to be your reality. We wrote this how-to book to help leaders like you and others succeed at getting important behaviors embedded into your organization's DNA.

What's the Solution? Consistent Vital Behaviors!

Ultimately, execution boils down to all the behaviors (actions) taken by employees every day. *The reality of execution is that nothing changes until people's behaviors change.* This is especially true at the front line for any change effort, where the day-to-day behaviors of leaders and associates make all the difference. That's where the rubber hits the road.

It's clearly impossible for any leader to oversee all the behaviors of every direct report. That would be world-class micromanaging, and it would drive employees toward the door. For leaders, it's obviously much easier to support direct reports in implementing a few mission-critical Vital Behaviors rather than micromanaging everything.

We have helped hundreds of organizations execute initiatives and supercharge results by focusing on Vital Behaviors. They are quite simply the key to superior performance.

Vital Behaviors
The vital few mission-critical behaviors that will dramatically improve targeted results when a large group of people make them habits.

Vital Behaviors Follow the 80/20 Rule

The 80/20 rule states that 80% of a result is produced by a small minority of causes (20%). When we apply this rule to behaviors, we see that out of everything we do in business and life, a small number (20%) of our actions have a big impact, accounting for 80% of the results we achieve.

The 80/20 rule was discovered by economist Vilfredo Pareto. In 1895 Pareto found that 80% of Italian land was owned by 20% of the people. He created mathematical models to describe this economic phenomenon. In 1941, quality expert Joseph M. Juran found that the 80/20 rule was a universal principle, applicable to a wide range of situations beyond economics, and was especially helpful in explaining quality issues. For example, he found that 80% of customer complaints were related to 20% of a company's products, or 20% of the steps in a work process were causing 80% of the defects. Everywhere he looked, he found that roughly 80% of outcomes stem from about 20% of causes.

Juran named this theory the Pareto Principle and developed a method to quantify the vital few causes that, if fixed, would lead to the biggest improvements in quality. He called the 20% big hitters the "vital few" and the remaining 80% the "trivial many." He found that he could make quality improvement easier and more effective by focusing on the 20%.

Richard Koch's seminal book, *The 80/20 Principle: Achieve More with Less* extended the application of the 80/20 rule beyond business to help millions of people succeed in personal life. For example, did you know that 80% of your happiness comes from 20% of the important decisions you've made? Through numerous examples, he showed how the 80/20 principle can vastly improve our happiness and effectiveness.

We now know that the 80/20 rule also applies to behaviors in organizations. Here's an example of how powerful it is when leaders and associates focus on a vital few behaviors rather than the trivial many.

On a project involving a telecommunications customer call center, thousands of associates underwent sales training, acquiring numerous new skills and behaviors. Four months later, sales had barely increased, and management was shocked when we told them that call center representatives were only asking for the sale in a mere 15% of customer interactions. This revelation prompted leaders to make "Asking for the sale" a Vital Behavior for call center reps. Remarkably, when this behavior was applied to 85% of customer calls, sales soared.

Why do Vital Behaviors produce remarkable results? When they become a focal point, leaders and associates can collectively keep an eye on whether people are doing them. This focused attention produces sustainable results more quickly. When Vital Behaviors become "treasured and measured," this spotlight on the vital few behaviors versus the trivial many simplifies behavior-powered improvements for everyone!

Consistent Behaviors Are Priceless— Inconsistent Behaviors Can Be Costly

The great news is that human behavior doesn't come with a price tag. Consistent behavior can be like a turbo boost for your organization, and it won't cost you anything extra. In contrast, inconsistent behavior can be an expensive stumbling block if you underestimate its importance in achieving effective execution.

You might hesitate to discuss specific behaviors with your team because you want to avoid micromanaging. So you hope they'll make the right choices on their own. Alternatively, you might turn a blind eye to inconsistent behavior because delivering constructive feedback makes you uncomfortable. But be cautious about disregarding this inconsistency. It can lead to significant costs. For example:

- When customers have a single, terrible customer experience, 67% of them will take their business elsewhere.

- In healthcare, Dr. Peter Pronovost developed and tested a 5-step checklist for preventing central line catheter infections. In 2010 he found that the steps in the checklist were followed less than 40% of the time, causing the loss of 28,000 lives per year nationwide and $2.3 billion in additional costs to treat avoidable complications.

- Employees crave recognition and appreciation—a seemingly small thing. When they don't get it, every major business result suffers—quality, productivity, engagement, retention. In spite of this, leaders seldom prioritize the simple behaviors of providing feedback and recognition.

Vital Behaviors Produce Remarkable Results

Behaviors are vital if they are the most important behaviors to do to produce a targeted result, yet they are often overlooked. How do you tell? If groups of people do Vital Behaviors more consistently, results improve. If inconsistency gets worse, results do too. This link between Vital Behaviors and results should be clear to everyone.

Below are examples of Vital Behaviors. They may sound obvious, but Vital Behaviors often are overlooked or ignored, to an organization's peril:

Vital Behavior: Handwashing by healthcare workers. Care providers wash their hands at the right times only about 30% of the time. (Surprised to hear that?) Every 10% increase in the Vital Behavior of "handwashing" results in a 6% reduction in hospital-acquired infections. If 100% of healthcare workers followed handwashing procedures, roughly 1 million lives would be saved each year in just the United States!

Vital Behaviors: Surfacing and tracking barriers. Years ago, a Behavior Science colleague of ours studied software development teams to see why some were more productive than others. The top teams came in on time and on budget. They met or even exceeded expectations. Why? It turned out they consistently did two Vital Behaviors.

First, when team members faced a barrier, they brought it up during the very next daily team meeting, rather than waiting to solve it themselves. And second, the team tracked and celebrated when barriers were surfaced.

High-performing teams surfaced barriers, big and small, *early* in the project, so they could be addressed quickly. Low-performing teams routinely surfaced barriers *late* in the game, especially big ones, creating rework and missed deadlines.

Vital Behaviors: Eating roots and talking about food. A global health organization was working in an area of the world where malnutrition was off the charts. The team on the ground saw that some families were able to keep their children well-nourished. How did these families do this when they experienced the same dire conditions others faced?

By observing and talking with them, the team uncovered the mission-critical things they were doing differently. These families were doing simple behaviors like talking daily about their food supply and who needed more food (and energy) to work. They also ate roots that were culturally shunned by most other families but provided key nutrients.

The team implemented a community-oriented, behavior-based change approach to help families spread those behaviors like wildfire. As the behaviors were adopted, the number of children and families that were malnourished dropped dramatically.

In all three of the examples above, the Vital Behaviors were linked to better results. If the people in these cases stopped doing these behaviors, or did them inconsistently, the results would suffer. That's the test for proving when behaviors are truly vital.

Vital Behaviors Can Help Resolve Diverse Challenges

Here are a few situations our clients and colleagues faced where Vital Behaviors dramatically improved the outcomes:

"Our agency-wide Vital Behaviors ensured that 50 people on our hospice care teams delivered the perfect care visit every time."

"Our company-wide Vital Behaviors first got 17,000 people to show up for work on time, then consistently do the vital things needed to make our railroad run on time."

"Our shift-wide Vital Behaviors got people to follow safety and quality procedures every time."

"Our nation-wide Vital Behaviors changed our national teen culture from one where heavy drinking was encouraged to one where alcohol abuse is now rare."

"Our contractor Vital Behaviors helped 4,000 temporary workers switch out 30,000 desktop computers globally, on time and on budget. They met the goal of replacing each machine in 45 minutes by focusing on targeted customer service behaviors, which eliminated rework and delays."

"Our company-wide Vital Behaviors aligned 29,000 flight attendants around the world to do the four things our frequent flyers said were the most important things they wanted in-flight to remain loyal to our airline."

"Our division-wide Vital Behaviors for leaders caused our results to soar when 85% of leaders consistently provided feedback and coaching to their direct reports."

"Our sales-specific Vital Behaviors doubled revenues for our small engineering firm when our sales reps started to take specific actions to 'own' their customer relationships over the entire project, not just during the sale."

Vital Behaviors Need to Be Customized for Your Organization

In his book, *The Checklist Manifesto: How to Get Things Right*, Dr. Atul Gawande illustrated how a simple checklist was used to dramatically improve surgical outcomes in eight very different hospitals across the world. The study, sponsored by the World Health Organization (WHO), involved hospitals ranging from those that are the very best in the world to some of the most resource-starved facilities in remote places.

A baseline study showed there would be substantial opportunity for improvement across all hospitals by increasing adherence to the checklist. This was especially true for six items related to Vital Behaviors that were needed to ensure patient safety (examples: Delivering antibiotics before surgery to prevent infections; accounting for all sponges at the end of the surgery to make sure none were left in the patient). On average, surgical teams missed at least one safety item for a staggering two-thirds of patients, regardless of whether their hospital was rich or poor.

During the three-month implementation of this two-minute checklist, surgical complications fell by 36%. Deaths decreased substantially by 47%. WHO estimated that this surgical checklist would save 500,000 lives every year if implemented worldwide. As a result of these findings, numerous countries have implemented the checklist, saving an untold number of lives.

Here's an interesting fact from that study. The original checklist started with 19 items. As it rolled out, each hospital customized the checklist to fit its unique conditions. Some changed the order of the items; others changed the terminology. A few added or subtracted items.

The researchers let this happen, as they knew the checklists would fail if they tried to dictate the items. People needed the freedom to adapt the checklist to make it their own. Regardless of the changes made to the starter checklist, all hospitals saw significant improvements in key outcomes after the checklists were implemented.

All organizations work the same way—they need to adapt Vital Behaviors to fit their unique circumstance. Here's another example to illustrate the point. We were teaching an internal group of performance improvement specialists about Vital Behaviors. We wanted them to see how Vital Behaviors for one organization differ from another, even though they both might have the same goals. We split them into two groups to observe two companies, sending one off to JCPenney and the other to Nieman Marcus. Their charge was to define the Vital Behaviors that constituted "great customer service" at each company. They also needed to find out how each measured success.

We arranged meetings with managers and employees at each store. We also gave our trainees plenty of time to observe customer-facing behaviors. To their surprise, they came back with vastly different lists of Vital Behaviors. JC Penney's floor personnel had Vital Behaviors that most of the trainees were used to seeing. It was the Vital Behaviors for Nieman Marcus that really shocked them—only a few in the group had ever experienced the world-class customer service that differentiates Nieman Marcus (see table).

Goal: "Provide Great Customer Service"

	JCPenney Sales Associates	Nieman Marcus Sales Associates
Sample Vital Behaviors	• Smile and greet customers in your area • Ask if customer needs help • Take customer to the merchandise they need • Guide customer to checkout area	• Offer to place special orders for customers • Arrange tailors, if needed • Give customer your personal business card to call anytime • Build personal rolodex of loyal customers & track their preferences
Success Metrics	• Increase customer satisfaction scores for the store	• Increase personal sales for each sales associate

As you see, Vital Behaviors reflect an organization's brand, policies, procedures, work processes, terms, and tools. You might start out with a set of Vital Behaviors that are evidence-based (proven to be effective based on current research), but no matter what, they will need to be customized to fit your unique situation and ensure your people own them.

Chapter 1 Summary

- Vital Behaviors are the few mission-critical behaviors that will dramatically improve targeted results when a large group of people make them habits.

- Consistent Vital Behaviors are the key to execution excellence and supercharging results.

- Inconsistent Vital Behaviors can be costly in terms of profitability, customer loyalty, productivity, employee retention, etc.

- Vital Behaviors reliably produce remarkable results.

- Vital Behaviors can solve diverse challenges at any level in an organization.

- Vital Behaviors need to be customized for your organization to reflect your brand, policies, procedures, work processes, terms, and tools, and to gain buy-in from your people.

2

How to Find Vital Behaviors in Your Organization

How many times have you heard a leader say,

"They know the goals. We gave them the tools and resources they need. We've broken down the work into tasks and timelines. We've even beefed up our performance management system and linked pay to outcomes. But we still aren't getting it done!"

Maybe this was once you. By now, are you thinking about areas where clear Vital Behaviors might help everyone get it done? If so, you are beginning to understand how valuable it will be if you can count on the *right* people to do the *right* things at the *right* times—every time. You see that Vital Behaviors can be your organization's supercharger. But where can you find Vital Behaviors?

Don't Look to Your Traditional Management Tools for Vital Behaviors

Every leader in every industry relies on traditional management tools to execute (see Figure 1). These tools are taught in business schools throughout the world and are learned on the job by leaders at all levels.

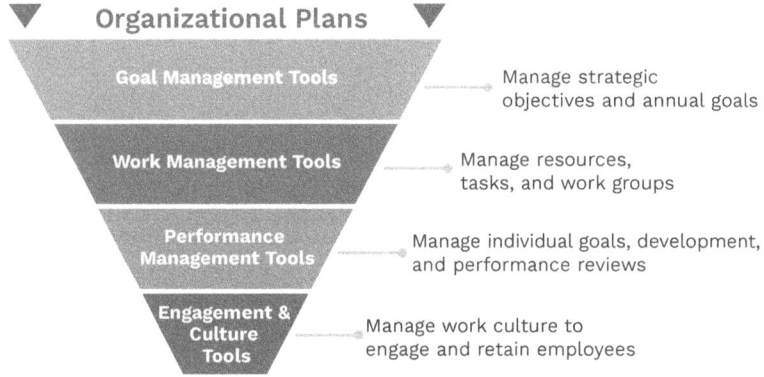

Figure 1

These traditional tools have obvious value by aiming people toward longer-term outcomes that can take weeks or months to achieve. But individual leaders must somehow cobble together all these management tools to execute plans in their areas on a daily basis. Leaders alone are responsible for helping direct reports see the links between their daily actions and the achievement of all the organizational goals. Unfortunately, they can't look to their existing management tools to make those links—they're missing.

As a leader, you need to create the connections between Vital Behaviors and the outcomes outlined in your organizational plans (e.g., strategic and business plans, project plans, sales plans, process improvement plans, work team plans). These links are shown in Figure 2.

Figure 2

You start by reviewing your organizational plans to identify which results suffer from unwanted or unproductive behavior variations. We call these Behavior-Powered Results because they will only be achieved if behavioral consistency occurs across lots of people. (Chapter 6 guides you through a process to help you find these Behavior-Powered Results.)

Your task is then to link the Behavior-Powered Results with the Vital Behaviors. By addressing these critical connections, you will make execution easier—and more reliable—for everyone. Employees will be grateful that you've provided a clear line-of-sight between their daily behaviors and business results. People like to know their contributions count!

Where Do You Find Vital Behaviors?

If you are wondering how to discover Vital Behaviors in your organization, here are seven ways.

1. **Look for obvious behaviors that should be more consistent.** Oftentimes, Vital Behaviors are things that people already know they need to do, but aren't doing each and every time—things related to safety, quality, reliability, etc. For example, maybe everyone has become lax about putting on personal protective equipment (PPE) before entering a dangerous worksite. Start by looking for these obvious behaviors that everyone knows are a problem, then use a check sheet to observe whether these behaviors are occurring when they

should be. This will provide some initial data to confirm whether they really are problems.

2. **Ask the people who do the work.** Because people on the frontline are so close to their work, they are best positioned to identify Vital Behaviors. Here's an example that proves this point. In one manufacturing project, we faced a significant challenge. Despite maintenance departments at 22 different sites diligently following their preventive maintenance schedules, machine downtime remained too high. This issue resulted in costly delays, amounting to hundreds of thousands of dollars in losses each time a machine went down. However, there was one mechanic who seemed to have a unique ability to identify machines that were on the verge of breaking down, even if they weren't scheduled for maintenance. So, what was his secret?

Every day, this mechanic would talk with the machine operators in his area. Together they would actively listen to the machines for any unusual or funny noises and closely examine the machine's output for any deviations from the norm. These two behaviors, listening for strange noises and monitoring output, were the keys to his success.

The client decided to test these Vital Behaviors with the 400 mechanics across all the sites. The results were remarkable. Machine downtime dropped significantly once these behaviors were adopted by the maintenance teams. Millions of dollars were saved.

The crucial point here is that these Vital Behaviors were only discovered by someone working on the frontline, a fellow mechanic. This made it easier for others at different sites to accept and implement them.

3. **Ask the experts.** Turn to Subject Matter Experts internally and externally to find best practices. We've been able to find starter sets of Vital Behaviors for almost every challenge our clients have faced in every industry. Look at research articles and call the authors to learn more about what they found that works. Call industry experts—they are everywhere—in universities, professional associations, government agencies, and especially in your organization's internal support departments. They will be happy to share what they've learned that works!

4. **Observe high and low performers.** Identify your high performers (top 10%) and low performers (bottom 10%). Spend time observing them to uncover key differences in their actions that lead to such varying outcomes. As you watch them perform tasks, you'll notice distinct behaviors that contribute to their success.

   An insightful example of observing performers comes from Dr. Neil Rackham's 1988 groundbreaking book, *SPIN Selling*. Dr. Rackham observed 35,000 sales calls across 27 countries to identify the Vital Behaviors necessary for successful major sales. In the realm of large, strategic sales, where customers are making substantial commitments of time, money, and resources, the dynamics differ greatly from smaller sales. In these high-stakes situations, customers are taking a considerable risk and placing significant trust in their salesperson.

   Dr. Rackham's findings showed that the lowest performing 10% of salespeople continued to employ traditional sales techniques that worked for smaller tactical sales, such as emphasizing features and benefits, addressing objections, and resorting to high-pressure closing tactics. However, these methods didn't prove effective in larger, strategic sales.

For major sales, the most successful salespeople did not just talk at customers and emphasize product or service features. Instead, they dedicated 70% of their time to asking questions and listening. The goal was to better understand the customer's true business challenges and the implications of solving them, or not. From this, Dr. Rackham created the sales process of SPIN selling: **S**ituation questions, **P**roblem questions, **I**mplication questions, and **N**eed-payoff questions.

Once these Vital Behaviors for major sales were trained and executed effectively, companies using SPIN Selling experienced an impressive average increase in sales volume of 17% compared to control groups. This approach is now being used by sales forces across the globe.

Obviously, you won't have to do 35,000 observations! However, we guarantee that you will learn a tremendous amount if you observe even a very small number of high and low performers and find out why they are doing things in a certain way. Just give it a try.

5. **Analyze your customer's journey.** Look for those "moments of truth" where key events in a customer's experience with your organization cause them to form a lasting positive or negative opinion about your brand. For example, filing a claim for a car wreck can turn into either a "moment of pain" or a "moment of joy," depending on how the insurance representative handles it. Consider whether associates consistently do the right things during your organization's key moments of truth.

Sometimes Vital Behaviors can be uncovered by examining customer survey results or conducting interviews and focus groups with customers. For a global airline, we used all three data gathering methods and found that frequent flyers wanted: (1) their elite status to be acknowledged by a flight attendant, (2) their call buttons to be answered quickly, (3) to be kept informed in-flight about delays and options, and (4) service recovery to happen quickly when things went wrong. When those behaviors started happening across 29,000 flight attendants globally, customer loyalty soared among these frequent flyers.

6. **Find "behavior hot spots" in your work processes.** Every organization has work processes that contain best practices, procedures, protocols, work standards, job aids, etc. But of all the things employees need to do, not all rise to the level of being vital because you can already count on them to happen. For example, when developing the 19-item surgical checklist we mentioned in Chapter 1, Dr. Atul Gawande did not include a seemingly critical step: Managing fire hazards in the Operating Room. These fires are so rare that they seldom contribute to the results he was after, which was to reduce the big global killers in surgery. Dr. Gawande's 19-item checklist instead focused on the behavior hot spots where behavior variability was leading to poor surgical outcomes.

We worked with one global company to add the Vital Behavior component to its Lean Program. They recognized that process changes require behavior changes to sustain improvements. Their mantra became, "Nothing changes until behavior changes."

After company teams redesigned their work processes, we asked everyone to place a red dot on the hot spots in the process where they thought people would not want to perform the step, or would not consistently adhere to the step. The red dots quickly concentrated around specific steps in the process and handoffs between departments. These behavior hot spots needed to be redesigned—or if that wasn't possible, the behaviors needed to be treated as Vital Behaviors so they could be managed until they became habits.

Sometimes we had to really probe to discover why people would not (or could not) do the process step to standard. We would find that the true behavior hot spot lay elsewhere in the company's other processes. For example, a cable company's call center developed a new process for handling customer calls. One process step was identified as a behavior hot spot: "Handle customer needs in one call to eliminate call-backs." Industry-wide, everyone was focused on this "first-call resolution" metric. If that could be achieved, customers would be happier and fewer reps would be needed to handle multiple, unnecessary repeat calls with customers.

We analyzed why call center reps had difficulty doing the first-call resolution step, and it became clear that they were not at fault. They were dealing with follow-up calls from customers who were angry about the service provided by the in-home cable installers. Complaints revealed that the installers were failing to do four Vital Behaviors: (1) let the customer know when they would arrive, (2) clean up any messes they made in the customer's home, (3) explain what they had installed or fixed, and (4) show the customer how to use the equipment. Once the installers started to execute these Vital Behaviors reliably, first-call resolution became the norm and call center staffing levels decreased to meet industry standards, with no behavior changes by call center reps. The lesson here? Sometimes the cause of behavior hot spots lies hidden elsewhere in the organization's cross-functional processes.

Several of our colleagues have continued to develop what our clients originally christened "Behavioral Lean Six Sigma." They've taken the red dot approach and developed it into sophisticated tools such as Behavior Annotated Flowcharts, where workflows and behavior management systems are integrated. These tools provide a great way to identify and embed Vital Behaviors into work processes.

7. **Look for "cornerstone behaviors" that are foundational to other behaviors.** Every parent has said to their teenager, "Call me if you've been out drinking and you need a ride home." Yet, when they call you at midnight to come get them, the natural temptation when they get in the car is to holler at them for drinking, rather than praising them for their behavior of calling you—the very cornerstone behavior you want to encourage. (The other behavior, drinking, can be dealt with in the morning when everyone is more clear-headed.)

The same thing plays out in organizations. When an employee comes to you with a problem, you can either thank them for bringing the issue to you, or you can shout, "Why didn't you tell me about this before?" Several of our clients have made it clear that two Vital Behaviors for everyone are "surfacing issues as soon as they occur" and "don't blame the bearer of bad news," because they are the cornerstone behaviors for fixing problems before it's too late.

Another striking example of cornerstone behaviors comes from a project we had with a vast national railroad. Keeping trains on schedule is always hard, and the CEO was innovating a new way for the entire rail system to operate on time. However, a major barrier existed: People weren't showing up to work on time, from top management to rail yard employees, and this was an ingrained bad habit. It would be impossible to run the railroad on time if people weren't ready to start their workday or shift on time.

So, we introduced a very simple Vital Behavior called "dressed and ready." This meant every employee had to arrive for work and be suited-up on time for the beginning of their shift or workday. An entire workforce of 17,000! We started this cornerstone behavior on a designated Monday. Everyone understood that "dressed and ready" would be heavily reinforced and transparently managed at all levels. And disciplinary procedures that had become lax over the years would be consistently applied from that day onward because "dressed and ready" was vital to the railroad's success. Once this cornerstone behavior became consistent, leaders gained confidence in their ability to work with employees to implement other Vital Behaviors essential for the organization's success.

Vital Behaviors Need to be Owned by the People in Your Organization

It's crucial to engage leaders, associates, internal and external customers, and other stakeholders in defining Vital Behaviors. These behaviors should not be prescribed or dictated by outsiders; they must be collaboratively identified by the group expected to implement them. Even for the surgical safety checklist discussed in Chapter 1, when everything at first seemed cut and dried, people still found important adjustments that needed to be made. You've got to allow that flexibility.

We've witnessed what happens when a static set of Vital Behaviors are imposed on employees. One healthcare consulting firm identified mission-critical behaviors that it said reliably improved patient satisfaction ratings. They even had years of data as proof. And these behaviors seemed like they would be common sense for healthcare workers. Examples include: (1) look the patient in the eyes and introduce yourself and your role, (2) create a positive impression of others on the healthcare team, (3) let the patient know what is happening and how long it will take, and (4) thank them for choosing your healthcare organization.

Managerial behaviors also were prescribed. Leaders were to "round" on patients and healthcare workers a certain number of times each month to gather behavioral data and provide feedback to employees on whether they were doing these behaviors. Next, leaders were responsible for writing personal notes to send to employees thanking them for doing the right things. Impressively, many healthcare organizations were transformed by implementing these behaviors as prescribed.

Yet time and time again we heard healthcare workers complain, "These behaviors don't fit our culture." When we came back months or years later, it's no surprise the behaviors had faded. Even Quint Studer, the creator of these behaviors, has changed his approach. In his new book, *Rewiring Hardwiring*, he now advocates letting leaders and healthcare workers customize Vital Behaviors dynamically over time so they can pick things that make sense to them and are doable.

In Chapter 8, you'll learn how to develop clear Vital Behaviors using a high-engagement process. The important thing to remember is that Vital Behaviors are dynamic, not static. They will change as people ask for more clarity and as conditions change. Vital Behaviors will also need to be updated if, after experimentation, you find they do not produce desired results. When people know they are not stuck forever with a rigid set of behaviors, they will be more willing to execute a starter set of Vital Behaviors that are roughly right and adjust as needed. That's the only way they will own them.

Chapter 2 Summary

- Traditional management tools help leaders achieve longer-term organizational goals.

- The missing links are Behavior-Powered Results and Vital Behaviors, which give employees a clear line-of-sight between their daily actions and business results.

- Vital Behaviors make it easier to execute organizational plans by focusing everyone on the mission-critical actions that need to happen consistently.

- Find Behavior-Powered Results by reviewing your organizational plans to see which results depend on consistent behaviors at scale:
  - Look for obvious behaviors that should be more consistent
  - Ask the people who do the work
  - Ask the experts
  - Observe high and low performers
  - Analyze your customer's journey
  - Find behavior hot spots in your work processes
  - Look for cornerstone behaviors that are foundational to other behaviors

- Vital Behaviors cannot be prescribed. They need to be customized and dynamically updated by people in your organization to ensure that the people who need to do these behaviors own them.

3

The 3 Pillars to Transform Vital Behaviors into Sustainable Habits

Carter Gets Thrown into the Deep Fryer

"I was sending out job applications everywhere, and then one day, this fast food place finally called me. I'd been stuck working with a groundskeeping company mowing grass, so I was psyched to be part of an actual team.

"In my first week, they had me glued to these training videos, and man, they were total snoozers. But I aced those easy tests. When I had some downtime, I tried to shoot the breeze with as many co-workers as I could, and they all seemed cool.

"At the end of that first week, my boss tells me I'm gonna start in the 'running' station, where we put together orders for the drive-thru and front counter. He said I'd pick up other stuff down the road. But let me tell ya, those first few weeks felt like getting thrown into the deep fryer.

"My boss started moving me around to new stations without any warning. He said I'd have assigned mentors to show me the ropes, but whenever I had a question, it's like my mentors either did it themselves or acted like I was bugging them. They'd point me to the job aids to read, but sometimes that stuff didn't match what I remembered from the videos.

"They told me I'd get my first review after 60 days, and that's when the raise and permanent job would kick in. I was all about getting some feedback during that time to lock in that raise. But my boss only seemed to notice when I screwed up, and he didn't hold back on letting me know. When I asked my co-workers for feedback, they pointed me back to my mentors or the boss, saying they were swamped.

"So, after 60 days rolled around, I only got half the raise I was aiming for. He told me I was moving too slow and talking too much. Then he slapped me with the afternoon shift, even though I told him I couldn't swing it when he hired me. That was the last straw, and I handed in my two-week notice.

"Thankfully, a buddy put me onto another fast food place that ran things a whole lot smoother. They laid out clear performance expectations every couple of weeks for the first three months. I knew exactly what skills I needed to learn and whether I was meeting standards. The best part is that I got an increase in pay as I learned new stuff. The managers and team members there were all about coaching and training, and they really had my back. When I told my managers I couldn't do afternoon shifts, they actually worked with me to sort it out. It was like a whole different ballgame, and I love every minute of my job."

The 3 Pillars to Build Good Habits and Succeed at Work

This fast food employee, Carter, has a lot in common with 100 million other employees in the United States. Regardless of a person's role or industry, only 21% of U.S. workers strongly agree their performance is managed in a way that motivates them to do outstanding work. At the most basic level, all people need three things from their leaders to form good habits and succeed at work. We call them the 3 Pillars because they are so essential (Figure 3).

THE 3 PILLARS FOR BUILDING GOOD HABITS

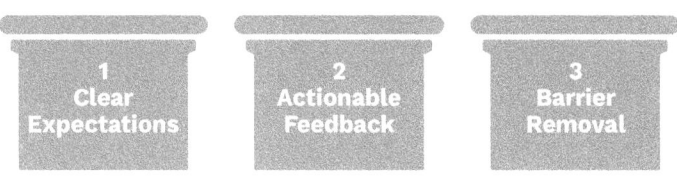

Figure 3

The 3 Pillars leaders need to provide to employees are:

1. **Clear Expectations** about what they need to do (the behaviors) to meet product/process standards and achieve goals.

2. **Actionable Feedback** about how well they are doing (weekly at a bare minimum!), with an emphasis on more positive than constructive feedback.

3. **Barrier Removal** so they can do desired behaviors.

Carter's leaders at the first fast food place didn't provide him with any of these essential elements. However, when he landed his second job, he got all three of these things. They were instrumental in turning him into a loyal, engaged employee who loved his job.

All 3 Pillars need to be strong for employees to build good habits and succeed at work. Believe it or not, a majority of employees do *not* receive these three things. Research by Gallup shows that **only 30%** of U.S. workers get all 3 Pillars. When Gallup correlated its survey results with actual organizational performance, they found that when **80%** of workers received this essential performance support, numerous performance indicators dramatically improved (Figure 4). These results also match decades of data we've gathered with our clients, as well as 50 years of research in the field of Organizational Behavior Management (OBM).

When 80% of workers get
THE 3 PILLARS FOR BUILDING GOOD HABITS
Performance Reliably Improves

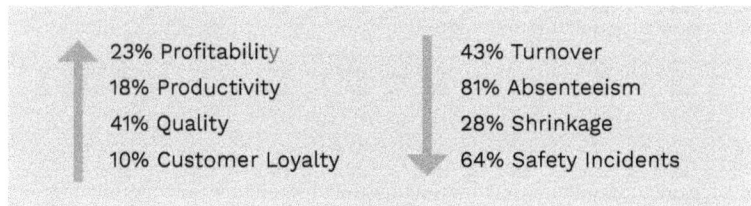

23% Profitability
18% Productivity
41% Quality
10% Customer Loyalty

43% Turnover
81% Absenteeism
28% Shrinkage
64% Safety Incidents

Figure 4

The data are clear: To improve performance, leaders need to provide this essential performance support to 80% or more of their direct reports. But how is this possible when so many things need to be done? By focusing on Vital Behaviors! When organizations focus on Vital Behaviors, it's possible to provide all 3 Pillars to **100%** of their people. You'll see the amazing results that are produced when this happens in the success stories presented later in this book.

How Do You Know If Vital Behaviors Have Become Personal Habits?

The 3 Pillars are needed for getting Vital Behaviors started and turning them into sustainable habits. But how will you know if people in your organization are getting behavioral traction on establishing enduring habits?

A colleague of ours, Dr. Laura Methot, conducted extensive research to identify the crucial turning point that signals when an individual has successfully transformed Vital Behaviors into reliable habits. Her study examined data from tens of thousands of observations of leaders at 25+

business and functional units worldwide, all in their first year of striving to adopt new leadership Vital Behaviors.

The results of her research revealed a significant insight: When an individual consistently engages in the targeted Vital Behaviors at least 85% of the time when the opportunity arises, they have reached a new level of habit strength that indicates durability and reliability of these behaviors. In collaboration with Dr. Methot we have devised a measurement tool to gauge whether Vital Behaviors have indeed transitioned into habits. This assessment is called Individual Habit Strength (Figure 5).

INDIVIDUAL HABIT STRENGTH

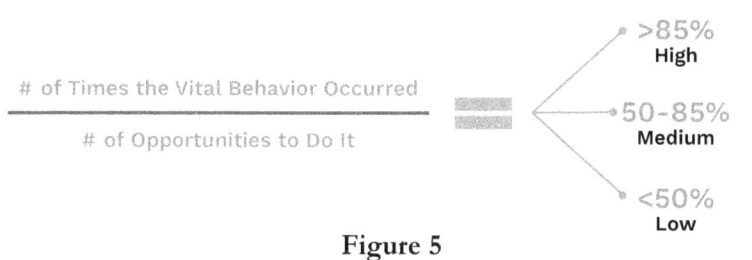

Figure 5

Let's swiftly calculate Individual Habit Strength in a restaurant setting. Suppose you aim to transform two Vital Behaviors of your waitstaff into a habitual practice: (1) clear a customer's table of dirty dishes within 5 minutes of guests finishing their meals, and (2) inquire if anyone desires dessert. Over a two-week period, if a server tends to 200 tables, they have a total of 200 chances to execute these behaviors. If they successfully carry out the behaviors only 80 times, their personal Individual Habit Strength is 80/200, or 40%, indicating weak habit strength, as depicted in Figure 5.

The good news is that you do not have to observe the server 200 times. You can get a good measure of habit strength by sampling the service they provide to 20 tables (10% of total opportunities) over this time period.

Why is understanding habit strength crucial? Because it guides your approach to supporting individuals in adopting Vital Behaviors. When a Vital Behavior hasn't yet become a habit for someone, you'll need to regularly provide the 3 Pillars to reinforce the importance of these desired behaviors. Conversely, if a waitstaff member consistently executes these behaviors correctly 85% of the time or more, it signifies that it's a strong habit for them. You might consider inviting them to become a coach for their colleagues who still need help developing these habits.

How Do You Measure Individual Habit Strength?

To gauge Individual Habit Strength, you need to gather solid behavioral data. Luckily, there are several ways you can do that without feeling like you are micromanaging people or trying to catch them doing something wrong. You can use what we call Vital Behavior spot checks. Figure 6 shows four different ways you can conduct spot checks.

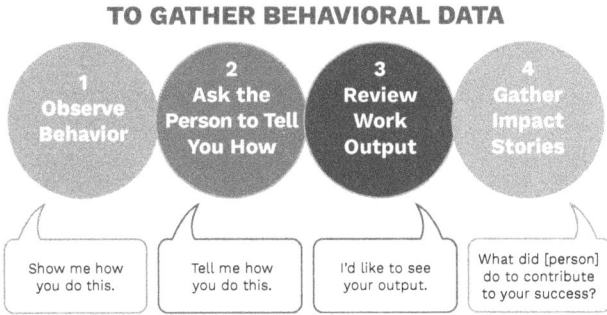

Figure 6

1. Directly observe the individual when they are doing the Vital Behaviors. Ask them, "Please show me what you do," or watch them in-the-moment to see how they naturally go about their work.

2. Ask the individual to tell you how they do the Vital Behaviors. Listen carefully to make sure they accurately describe what they need to do.

3. Review the work output (documentation, products, etc.) the individual produced by doing the Vital Behaviors. Engage the person by talking it through with them to make sure they can accurately evaluate the quality of their own work output.

4. Gather impact stories from others about what happened when the individual did (or did not) do the Vital Behaviors. What was the impact of their behavior? Did it help (or hinder) success? Then share those stories with the individual.

You can collect behavioral data using all four methods. We recommend that you use a checklist so you can count the number of times the Vital Behaviors were done correctly when the opportunity arose. Once you have the behavioral data, you can assess an individual's Habit Strength to see whether it's high, medium, or low, and then apply the 3 Pillars accordingly.

How Will You Know When Habits Have Become Embedded in Your Organization's DNA?

When a core percentage of your people develop high habit strength around a set of Vital Behaviors, you reach a tipping point where the culture changes. The Vital Behaviors become embedded habits, or "just the way we do things here." When Vital Behaviors achieve this norm, we call them hardwired or cultural habits.

How can you tell when that tipping point has been reached? Dr. Methot found that when at least 85% of people display strong Individual Habit Strength for Vital Behaviors, that's the crucial point: That's when a core percentage of the population have transformed these behaviors into cultural habits that persist over time.

Most leaders we know are impatient. They want to know how long it will be before the tipping point is reached! When can they sigh relief, knowing that new habits are embedded in their organization's DNA?

To find out, lead author Julie Smith collaborated with Dr. Mikel Harry, widely recognized as the co-creator and chief architect of Six Sigma. Six Sigma assesses process adherence over the long-term by looking at defects per million opportunities. Julie aimed to develop a similar metric to gauge behavioral adherence over the long-term across an organization. Her goal was to create a single, clear metric to enable leaders to see when new habits had taken hold.

Together, Julie and Mikel analyzed a decade of data. These data came from several organizations that had implemented behavior-based improvements. Their initial goal was to discover if the Six Sigma metric, which captures defects, could be converted into a positive metric that focused on successes. Julie felt strongly that the ultimate metric needed to be achievement-oriented. Luckily, they found that all the theories, assumptions, and mathematical equations of process adherence also held true for behavioral adherence.

Their next step was to develop a straightforward method to measure Organizational Behavior Momentum (Figure 7).

Figure 7

We won't bore you with the math. The concept is simple: We start by calculating how quickly Key Performers are adopting Vital Behaviors over a specified time period (the Rate of Improvement). Then we multiply that by the percentage of Key Performers who have achieved high Individual Habit Strength. That number tells us whether we've achieved the tipping point and have a critical mass of people driving the adoption of Vital Behaviors. As Dr. Methot said, the tipping point comes when at least 85% of a group develops high Individual Habit Strength for Vital Behaviors.

When speed of improvement is multiplied by the mass of people who actually have changed and are supporting it, the resulting number is what we've named Organizational Behavior Momentum. We are developing this standardized metric to help leaders and associates assess the current level of cultural force behind turning Vital Behaviors into sustainable habits. Furthermore, we have begun to correlate the Organization Behavior Momentum metric with Rate of Improvement for results. It is proving to be a valuable predictive indicator of how long it will take your organization to embed new habits, and ultimately achieve its Behavior-Powered Results.

Much work remains to further test and develop our Organization Behavior Momentum equation. In the future, our plan is to validate this Behavior Momentum as the single metric that will help you gauge how quickly your organization can hit that tipping point (and desired results). And you will be able to quickly calculate that metric through random observations of Vital Behaviors. Stay tuned!

Sustainable Cultural Habits Are Nurtured by All

So, why is it that when 85% of your people are doing Vital Behaviors regularly it becomes the tipping point? It's because you and your team have created a culture where enough people actively (1) help other team members understand the expectations, (2) provide feedback, and (3) remove barriers to help them do the right things. In other words, lots of people are providing the 3 Pillars, not just leaders. Cultural momentum has been built to support these behaviors, and it would be extremely hard for any individual to stop that momentum.

Think about it. Have you ever transitioned to a new work organization where the cultural norms and habits differed from your previous one? For example, perhaps everyone consistently arrives on time and well-prepared for meetings, while your previous organization was more relaxed about these aspects. It's remarkable how quickly you adapt to these new habits, especially when your new colleagues encourage you to be punctual and prepared. They might even offer you assistance because they understand that your success contributes to their own.

You immediately see there is cultural momentum to support the Vital Behaviors related to effective meetings, so you get on board and let your old sloppy ways go. It would be useless for you to try to get your new colleagues to chill. It isn't going to happen! These well-structured meeting behaviors are already embedded in their organization's DNA.

Let's look to DuPont for an example of habits that have been hard-wired for decades and nurtured by all. If you've ever visited a DuPont facility, you'd quickly notice that everyone highly values safe behaviors—and it shows. We've witnessed a plant manager picking up a piece of trash in a stairwell so no one trips and falls on it.

Their commitment to safety is evident in the impressive safety results they achieve. In 2019, across their 182 sites, a remarkable 73% managed to achieve zero injuries. DuPont is widely recognized for its dedication to making safe behaviors a part of every employee's daily routines.

In communities where DuPont employees live, it's easy to spot them because they take safety seriously, even off the job. You'll see them wearing personal protective equipment like safety glasses and hearing protection while mowing their lawns. Out of real concern, they will kindly nudge their neighbors to take safety precautions if they see something awry. At work or at home, if someone tries to get them to cut corners and skip the safety procedures, they won't do it.

DuPont's reputation for safety excellence is so renowned that other organizations regularly seek their guidance on how to replicate their success. So, what's their secret sauce that they share with others? There are two reasons for their success. First, DuPont teaches organizations how to use something akin to the 3 Pillars to establish safe habits. It's no surprise that these pillars play a crucial role in their safety success.

Second, DuPont expects everyone to use these 3 Pillars to nurture safe habits for themselves and others. When it comes to safety, there is no organizational hierarchy. For example, everyone is responsible for stopping unsafe acts immediately and then encouraging safe acts. One of the authors witnessed a meeting where an executive called into a project team meeting to see how their work was progressing. Everyone could clearly hear the background noise on the call. One of the project team members said, "I just have to ask, for your own safety, are you calling from your car while driving? If so, we can wait to talk." The executive thanked the person and said he would call back in 10 minutes once he arrived at his destination. Now that's true ownership of cultural habits by both the frontline employee and the executive!

To sustain habits, everyone needs to help each other get clear about Vital Behaviors, provide in-the-moment feedback, and help remove barriers to doing it right. Everyone needs to become an "Ally" in helping each other change behaviors until they become habits that stick.

Leaders Are Pivotal to Building Habit Strength

Every organization we've worked with claims, "Safety is job #1." But if so, why don't all organizations have a safety culture like DuPont's? As you might have guessed, even though everyone is involved in safety at DuPont, it all comes down to consistent leadership of the safety culture. Our colleague, Dr. Judith Komaki, has spent her life researching the behaviors of leaders who produce extraordinary results like DuPont has. Dr Laura Methot also quantified the link between leader behaviors and business outcomes. Both of our colleagues found that performance-based leaders consistently demonstrate the following Vital Behaviors, which we turned into an acronym so it will be memorable for any leader:

The CORE Vital Behaviors for Leaders

- **C**larify expectations of Vital Behaviors and work outputs.

- **O**bserve and monitor Vital Behaviors and work outputs.

- **R**einforce (or redirect) Vital Behaviors using actionable feedback.

- **E**liminate barriers to Vital Behaviors and work outputs.

You'll notice that these CORE Vital Behaviors for Leaders directly overlap with the 3 Pillars. These are the Vital Behaviors you will need your leaders to do consistently if you are to achieve any Behavior-Powered Result you've set your sights on. You can customize them to make them your own, or add a few other things you think are important. For example, one company added the following Vital Behavior, "Seek feedback for yourself to be a role model." However you modify these four CORE Vital Behaviors for Leaders, remember that they are absolutely the mission-critical behaviors your leaders need to do to execute any Vital Behavior Blueprint.

Chapter 3 Summary

- There are 3 Pillars that every employee needs to build good habits and succeed at work: (1) clear expectations, (2) actionable feedback, and (3) barrier removal.

- Only 30% of workers in the U.S. get these 3 Pillars. When 80% of workers get these 3 Pillars, a variety of performance indicators reliably improve, as well as employee satisfaction and engagement.

- It's too hard for supervisors to provide these 3 Pillars for every employee responsibility. Focusing on Vital Behaviors makes it doable.

- Individual Habit Strength is a key metric for measuring whether Vital Behaviors have become an organizational or cultural habit.

- Individual Habit Strength is considered to be High when a person does the Vital Behavior more than 85% of the time when the opportunity arises, Medium when the Vital Behavior occur between 50–85% of the time, and Low when the behavior occurs less than 50% of the time.

- Habits become embedded in an organization's DNA when 85% of the targeted population achieves high Individual Habit Strength.

- Habits are sustained when everyone in a culture nurtures them by providing the 3 Pillars to each other.

- Leaders are pivotal to building habit strength. They need to do the four CORE Vital Behaviors for Leaders to support everyone in behavior change

    - **C**larify expectations of Vital Behaviors and work outputs.

    - **O**bserve and monitor Vital Behaviors and work outputs.

    - **R**einforce Vital Behaviors (or redirect) Vital Behaviors using actionable feedback.

    - **E**liminate barriers to Vital Behaviors and work outputs.

4

Move Beyond Top-Down Management to Build Engaged Ally Networks

Behavior Change Is Easier with Allies

"We thought we were doing the right things when we rolled out a Corporate Health and Wellness program to a group of remote workers. We added exercise rooms to each of their small workspaces. We got rid of the deep fat fryers in the kitchen to help remove temptation. Stuff like that.

"In hindsight, we should have known they would be PO'd! We almost had a mutiny on our hands. They complained bitterly, sharing messages like, 'GTH, as long as we do our job, the company has no right to intrude into our personal health,' and technically they were right.

"But we still had a big problem. This group worked two weeks on and two weeks off in a remote location. For shift changeovers, we had to transport the crews on helicopters into dangerous, windy conditions. Most of the guys were big, so we had to take two helicopters. If they weighed in the normal range, we would have needed only one. That alone would have reduced our safety risk.

"I turned to our behavioral experts to figure out what to do. Thank goodness I had them at my side. Together we repositioned the program as a safety program, which is what it really was for these workers. We helped them see that their health was as strategically and personally important as any other safety process or procedure we had. As leaders, we added health and wellness topics into our standup safety meetings. That cemented the fact that this was a safety issue for everyone.

"We knew we couldn't make it mandatory for them to make healthy lifestyle choices. Instead, there were three Vital Behaviors we felt strongly we needed to encourage over the first year to change our culture:

"Track your numbers. We educated everyone about the importance of tracking the top five metrics that are predictive of future health problems like diabetes and heart disease. Those numbers are glucose, cholesterol, triglycerides, waist circumference, and blood pressure.

"Establish a relationship with a primary care doctor. Everyone was challenged to select a provider to be their quarterback for all their health needs. We talked about why this was so important.

"Try using one or more of the corporate resources. We had hundreds of health and wellness resources available to employees, and many ways to earn points for healthy activities. We asked everyone to take a look. During Health and Wellness Safety meetings, we set aside time for people to share what they learned.

"As you can imagine, the more we started learning about health and wellness, the more we started talking about it beyond the safety meetings. And the more we began to encourage one another for trying new things such as different ways to prepare meals or reduce stress. We also removed some of the barriers we had inadvertently put in place. For example, it turns out the exercise rooms were above the bunkrooms. No one exercised because they didn't want to wake up their team members. So, we moved the exercise rooms.

"Because of privacy concerns, we never knew who had done the three behaviors—unless the person decided to share. But slowly, you could see the light bulbs go on and people begin to make changes. For once, those changes were applauded by their teammates, not laughed at.

"We celebrated about a year later when we learned that most shift changeovers could be accomplished with one helicopter because we met the weight limits. That felt great! As Allies, we had accomplished something together that we never could or would have done alone.

"During the second year, the crews voluntarily chose to do Vital Behaviors that would engage their families in this process. It was so rewarding to see them 'own' health and wellness for themselves, other team members, and their families."

Top-Down Management Can't Produce Sustainable Behavior Change— Ally Networks Are Needed

As shown in the story above, the traditional approach of top-down management, where bosses dictate everything, doesn't cut it when it comes to establishing long-lasting habits in an organization. Sure, a leader might get everyone to change their behavior for a short while, but once they're out of the picture, people tend to revert to their old ways. People have even learned to wait out implementing new strategic initiatives to see if their executives are going to stay the course. This cycle repeats across various industries.

Simply relying on leaders isn't enough to make habits stick in a company. For Vital Behaviors to truly become ingrained habits, they need support from a wide range of people, not just those in charge. It's much easier for individuals to change their behavior when they have a network of Allies backing them up.

This concept isn't new; it's something we often see in our personal lives. Many of us naturally have developed our own support networks. Think about it—how many times have you asked a friend to remind you to hit the gym or encouraged them to make healthier choices? Most people have a handful of supportive individuals like this in their lives, and it's for a good reason.

Who Are Allies?

> **Allies**
> Allies are people who are willing to help Key Performers do the necessary Vital Behaviors because they too have a vested interest in achieving the Behavior-Powered Results. They provide support that Key Performers find meaningful and important.

Allies can emerge from various sources. While leaders and team members are often seen as natural Allies, the scope can extend far beyond them. Trusted colleagues, peers, customers, stakeholders, esteemed community leaders, and even family members can all serve as Allies.

The crucial factor lies in identifying the groups whose feedback and support hold the most significance for Key Performers. For instance, in a school environment where teachers are the Key Performers, principals might assume they would be the most influential Allies in assisting teachers with Vital Behaviors. However, when teachers were consulted, they disagreed. They believed that students would offer the most valuable feedback and support.

Why did teachers hold this view? Because students interacted with them daily, could observe their actions in realtime, and provide frequent feedback. Additionally, teachers genuinely cared about their students' opinions. Their primary motivation for becoming teachers was to help students succeed, not solely to please their principals. Teachers felt that incorporating student input was essential for their professional growth. Consequently, they decided that students would constitute their primary Ally Group, with principals being designated as a secondary Ally Group.

What's an Ally Network?

You can intentionally create similar support networks at work to help people succeed at widely varied things. For example, you might create a network to master the skills needed to make major presentations, or one to walk every day at noon. We call each one an Ally Network.

> **Ally Network**
> Connects people who share mutual goals to support one another in turning Vital Behaviors into sustainable habits. Allies provide 3 Pillars needed to succeed: (1) Clear Expectations, (2) Actionable Feedback, and (3) Barrier Removal.

How Does an Ally Network Work?

An Ally Network has five components (Figure 8).

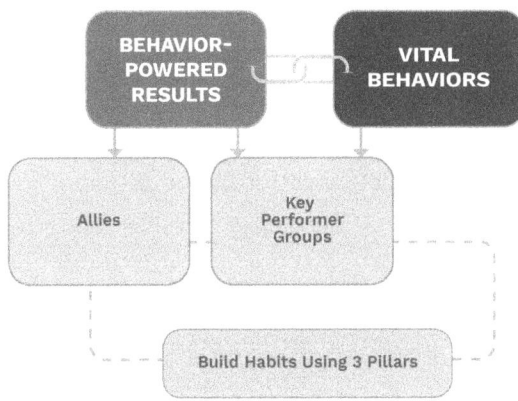

Figure 8

Behavior-Powered Results. People in the network come together because they all want to achieve shared goals, and they understand that behavioral consistency will help achieve those goals.

Key Performer Groups. These are the logical groupings of people whose behaviors most impact those results.

Vital Behaviors. These are the mission-critical behaviors each Key Performer Group needs to do to move the needle on the results. Vital Behaviors are linked to the results.

Allies. Leaders are always Allies, but they are not the only ones. Allies include others who have a mutual, vested interest in achieving the Behavior-Powered Results and are willing to help Key Performers in doing the Vital Behaviors.

Build Habits using the 3 Pillars. This is the ongoing, realtime support (Ally assists) that Allies provide to Key Performers:

- **Pillar 1: Clear Expectations.** Allies stay aligned with Key Performers regarding performance expectations (including clarity on desired Behavior-Powered Results, Vital Behaviors, and work output requirements).

- **Pillar 2: Actionable Feedback.** Allies frequently give Key Performers individualized, actionable feedback, celebrate progress, and redirect actions when needed.

- **Pillar 3: Barrier Removal.** Allies help Key Performers quickly resolve human performance barriers to enable execution.

The Ally Network focuses everyone on Vital Behaviors, which gives Allies an easy way to provide Key Performers with the 3 Pillars. This support is critical to helping everyone build and sustain new habits in organizations—and mutually achieve the Behavior-Powered Result.

Ally Networks Make It Easier for Everyone to Establish Habits

The story shared at the beginning of this chapter illustrates the power of collective behavior change compared to individual efforts. Who would have imagined that a group of remote workers could come together to exercise, adopt healthier eating habits, and ultimately shed enough weight to enhance the safety of their transportation to worksites? Such a transformation would have been improbable if they had attempted it alone.

By aligning Vital Behaviors with strategic safety objectives and fostering collaboration, these behaviors gradually took root. The formation of an Ally Network facilitated this process, making it easier for everyone involved. Leaders no longer needed to forcefully promote corporate programs, and employees were relieved of the stress from undertaking tasks solo or engaging in activities they were hesitant about.

Chapter 4 Summary

- Behavior change is easier when people do it together rather than alone.

- Top-down management can't produce sustainable behavior change.

- Allies are people who are willing to help Key Performers do the necessary Vital Behaviors. They can emerge from many sources, not just leadership.

- Ally Networks connect people who share mutual goals to support one another in realtime to turn Vital Behaviors into sustainable habits.

- Ally Networks make it easier for everyone to establish habits by providing each other with the 3 Pillars: (1) Clear Expectations, (2) Actionable Feedback, and (3) Barrier Removal.

5

Quick Start Guide to the 5 Steps for Building a Vital Behavior Blueprint

> **Vital Behavior Blueprint**
> A powerful 5-Step process for aligning Vital Behaviors with organizational goals and engaging an Ally Network to help turn these behaviors into habits at scale.

How Do You Build a Vital Behavior Blueprint?

Always engage Allies, from the front line to top leadership, to build your Blueprint. Reassure them that getting the Blueprint roughly right is good enough to get started. This is a dynamic process. The data will tell you if you are on track, and you can adjust the Vital Behaviors and feedback loops as you learn more.

To build your Vital Behavior Blueprint, follow our 5 Steps described in Figure 9.

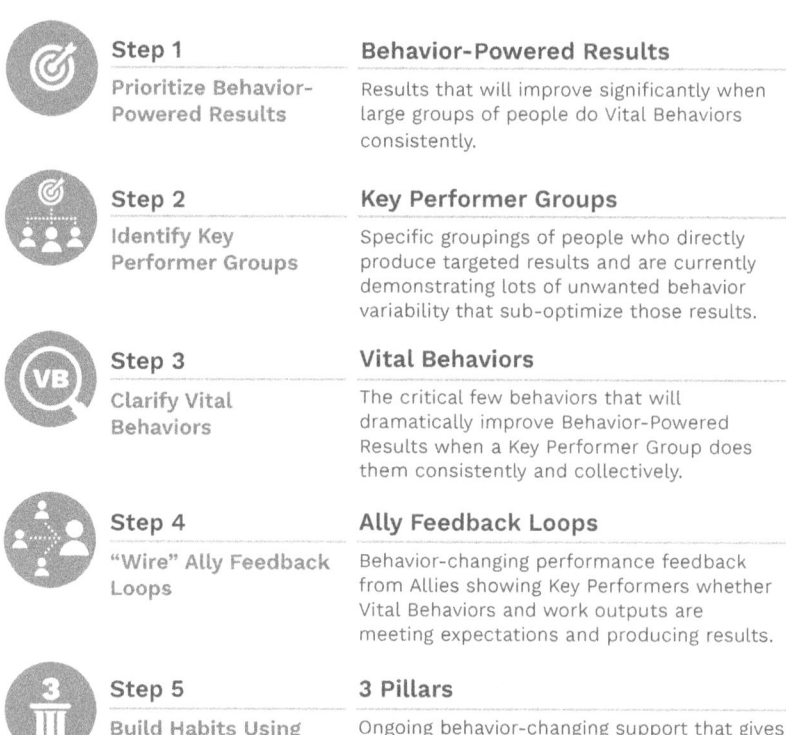

Figure 9

Example of a Vital Behavior Blueprint That Drove Positive Business Outcomes at "Cure Quest"

In the biopharmaceutical industry, the old sales model—in-person reps visiting doctors' offices—stopped working many years ago. This shift was due to new regulations and increasing mergers of physician offices into health systems. Not only did this change affect sales, but biopharma companies were losing their critical ears-to-the-ground through which sales reps gathered valuable intelligence about customers and patients:

- Why providers prescribed their medicines—or chose a competitor.

- Why patients filled a prescription and followed the treatment protocol as designed—or not.

- Whether the medicine had the intended health outcome—or not.

So here is what happened at Cure Quest (a fictitious name). In 2007, Don Curlew (a pseudonym) became the CEO. Don seemed like an odd choice, because he was neither physician nor researcher. Instead, his background was in managing and leading non-healthcare companies. But with his business expertise, Don knew that Cure Quest had to find alternative ways to access and learn from providers and patients. If it couldn't, sales would suffer, and most importantly, it would never achieve its mission: To create groundbreaking ways to restore health and save lives.

Don kicked off a strategic initiative called Patient and Customer Centricity. The purpose was to help all employees see that Cure Quest's future depended on everyone taking responsibility for developing customer and patient engagement strategies. The sales reps could no longer do it alone.

Don hired one of the Big Three management consultancies to create tools for employees to use to develop New Commercial Models. These tools laid out specific ways to listen to and learn from customers and patients. The goal was for everyone to capture significant implications for purchasing decisions and to see how Cure Quest could adjust its products and services to add even more value. For example, did patients need help getting to cancer treatments, or more assistance post-treatment? Did physicians need consulting support to adjust the layout of their facilities to deliver new treatments?

All of this seemed like the perfect start to a transformational effort—except one barrier quickly arose: Skeptical employees at all levels said this was a big ask, and they wanted proof that the Top 100 leaders were serious about it.

Thus, Don engaged co-author Julie Smith and her colleagues to develop a Vital Behavior Blueprint for executive leaders. The goal was to show the organization that its Top 100 leaders were aligned and committed to Patient and Customer Centricity. Here is how they followed the 5 Steps to build their Vital Behavior Blueprint:

Step 1: Prioritize Behavior-Powered Results. The ultimate goal was to increase sales of medicines that improved health outcomes for patients.

Step 2: Identify Key Performer Groups. The first group was Cure Quest's Top 100 leaders, because they showed high variability in demonstrating their concerted commitment toward Patient and Customer Centricity.

Step 3: Clarify Vital Behaviors. After interviews at all levels, people agreed that the Top 100 would clearly demonstrate their commitment to Patient and Customer Centricity if they did three Vital Behaviors consistently:

> **Three Vital Behaviors for Top 100 Leaders:**
> - Meet with one major customer quarterly to find out what they need from Cure Quest.
> - Sponsor a team to map the patient journey for a medicine and implement ways to make the journey easier for patients.
> - Talk about new learnings from customers at the beginning of every business review meeting to inform the financials. (In the past, only the financials were discussed.)

Step 4: "Wire" Ally Feedback Loops. The Top 100 leaders became Allies to each other and shared monthly memos of their learnings. This opened up everyone to feedback by peers, which is usually hard to accomplish at the executive level. Don provided short, individualized feedback to each of the monthly memos, so the Top 100 knew he was watching and appreciated their efforts.

Step 5: Build Habits Using 3 Pillars. Here are examples of how Allies used the 3 Pillars to help each other adopt Vital Behaviors:

- **Clear Expectations.** The Top 100 found the Vital Behaviors to be very clear—because they helped develop them. Don wisely did not prescribe exactly how they went about each behavior. Instead, he encouraged them to find creative ways to do the Vital Behaviors and share their successes and setbacks.

- **Actionable Feedback.** As mentioned, the Top 100 gave feedback to each other after reading the monthly update memos. In addition, the company's internal coaches were assigned to leaders to provide realtime feedback based on each leader's unique needs. These coaches sometimes went on customer visits and attended business review meetings.

- **Barrier Removal.** Each of the Top 100 faced very individualized barriers. Some didn't know what to say to patients they met while mapping the patient journey. Others avoided meeting with customers because they feared stepping on the toes of their salespeople. A few didn't know what to do when no one contributed customer stories at a business review meeting. The HR internal coaches played a critical role in helping each leader develop their own plans for overcoming their barriers. In some cases, they provided scripted prompts to get discussion started. In others they asked peers to offer tips if the leader was open to it.

The Patient and Customer Centricity initiative was extremely successful. Innovative commercial models were developed. Sales increased. Most importantly, the organization transformed itself from being internally focused to market-driven, resulting in Cure Quest creating one of the largest, self-originated R&D pipelines in the industry.

What's Next in Your Vital Behavior Blueprint Journey?

The next section of this book describes how to complete each of the 5 Steps. Throughout each step, we provide an example of the Vital Behavior Blueprint being constructed for a hospice agency, illustrating how straightforward it can be for you to create your Blueprint.

Want more tools?
Access our **HUB** on page 211 to get free *Vital Behavior Blueprint Templates* and more.

Chapter 5 Summary

- There are 5 Steps for building a Vital Behavior Blueprint:

  - Step 1: Prioritize Behavior-Powered Results.

  - Step 2: Identify Key Performer Groups.

  - Step 3: Clarify Vital Behaviors.

  - Step 4: "Wire" Ally Feedback Loops.

  - Step 5: Build Habits Using 3 Pillars.

- A Vital Behavior Blueprint can be developed for Key Performers at any level of an organization, including executives, as described in the Cure Quest case.

BUILD A VITAL BEHAVIOR BLUEPRINT IN 5 STEPS

How to Embed Mission-Critical Habits into Your Organization's DNA

Now that you have a grasp of the fundamentals, this section guides you through the process of constructing a Vital Behavior Blueprint. The ultimate goal of a Vital Behavior Blueprint is to build a culture where Vital Behaviors become second nature. As you know by now, extraordinary results come from ordinary actions done consistently.

We distilled the essential steps you need to take (and avoid!) to develop the Blueprint efficiently and quickly align the right stakeholders around it. In the following five chapters, you'll see how a hospice care organization built a Vital Behavior Blueprint. At the end of each chapter, we share an example of the output from a project team at the hospice care organization.

But first, let's introduce you to Darlene, the CEO of the hospice organization. You'll learn why she felt a Vital Behavior Blueprint was needed to help improve the quality of life for her care teams and the patients and families they served.

Darlene's Despair

Darlene was perplexed.

"I should have been overjoyed. After all, our team had accomplished an incredible feat. We had doubled the average daily patient census of our hospice care agency over the past year. But it didn't feel good. Not with the mountain of bad news that lay before us."

Indeed, the overall numbers were dismal: Satisfaction scores from families had declined significantly, and staff turnover increased dramatically and was now well above the industry average. Worst of all, rather than rely on our staff for support, panicked family members called 911, which often resulted in an ambulance ride to the emergency department for critically ill patients. That last one really bothered Darlene:

"No matter how many times I remind the care teams: 'No hospice patient wants to spend a single hour in the emergency room during their last days on earth,' it still happens too often. And it's almost always unnecessary. We can avoid it by better-preparing families on what to expect and how to help their loved ones. They call the ambulance because they get scared."

Payors recognized this too and docked Darlene's agency reimbursement $600 every time it happened, which eroded the already razor-thin profitability of her agency. Darlene admitted she'd had moments of self-pity, thinking, "It's not fair! I've done everything I know to lay the foundation for growth." Truly, her attempts were valiant:

- She brought in an expert to train staff in best practices for creating the perfect care visit.

- She invested in a new practice management system and outfitted care team members with tablet computers so they could more easily track and manage every patient visit.

- She added more staff so patients and families had ready access to spiritual advisors and social workers.

All of these were costly solutions, yet none worked in the way she had hoped. Darlene and her staff wondered how things had slipped so far, so fast. What in the world was going on?

When the agency was smaller, Darlene had done ride-alongs to see for herself how patient visits were going. So, Darlene hit the road to see for herself what was happening. She observed 10 random patient visits, either in-person or via video-calling. Her son had cautioned, "Mom, you know all your employees will be on their best behavior. You're the CEO! And you won't even be undercover." Yet Darlene was still surprised and dismayed by what she witnessed.

The steps in the perfect care visit training were being implemented haphazardly. For instance, only 60% of the staff actually counted the medications and supplies a patient had on hand, as they were supposed to do. The other 40% of staff simply asked patients or caregivers, "Do you have enough medicines and other supplies?" and accepted the answer.

Obviously, verifying the supplies on hand was extremely important. After all, the supplies were there to make the patient as comfortable as possible. When loved ones saw the patient was in pain and necessary supplies were gone, they were more likely to call an ambulance or call her agency for after-hours support. Such support was expensive because it often involved paying staff overtime to respond. It also caused undue stress for patients and families.

After completing the ride-alongs, Darlene could see clearly that people had all the tools they needed to create the perfect care visit. But they just weren't doing the right behaviors 100% of the time. They were not yet habits.

Darlene was ready to dive in and build her own Vital Behavior Blueprint. She launched her project team, a group of people who collectively could provide a comprehensive perspective about the reality of care visits and the business needs. The team included:

Executive sponsors. Darlene (CEO) and Juan (COO), both innovators who wanted to create a legacy as the region's best hospice provider.

Project team lead. Laila, Director of Training and Development, a high-potential candidate with great communication skills and a powerful network of people across the organization who trusted her.

Project team members. Respected care team members who consistently delivered perfect care visits: Two nurses, two nursing aids, one social worker, one chaplain.

Caregivers of patients who had passed. Two people who represented families that had high and low satisfaction ratings for the hospice services they received.

She challenged the project team to create a Vital Behavior Blueprint that would ensure the perfect care visit happened every visit. She asked them to capture their output for each step in the Blueprint template shown on the next page. She felt that this Blueprint would provide an easy way to communicate the plan with everyone.

The blank Vital Behavior Blueprint shown on the next page is the very same one that Darlene's team used to start building their Blueprint. In this part of our book, we will describe how to do each of the 5 Steps, then show you the outcome of that Step for Darlene's team. (This will prepare you to build your own Vital Behavior Blueprint!)

VITAL BEHAVIOR BLUEPRINT TEMPLATE

Step 1
Behavior-
Powered
Results

Step 2
Key Performer
Groups

Step 3
Vital
Behaviors

Vital Behaviors:
1.
2.
3.
4.
5.
6.
7.

Step 4
Ally Feedback Loops

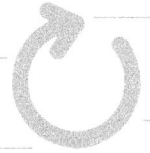

Step 5
3 Pillars

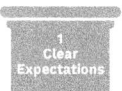
1
Clear
Expectations

2
Actionable
Feedback

3
Barrier
Removal

Top Barriers to Remove:

6

STEP 1:
Prioritize Behavior-Powered Results

Behavior variability can be a silent killer of business results. Behavior consistency of the right behaviors is the cure. Step 1 in building your Vital Behavior Blueprint is to identify which results you want to elevate to a new level of performance by focusing on Vital Behaviors.

You need to be selective, because not all results can be improved using a behavior-powered approach. Sometimes you do need new tools or equipment, or more staffing. But, if you are not seeing the results you want, look at the consistency of your team's actions as a possible root cause of poor performance. If you are seeing lots of unwanted and unproductive behavior variability, then these results are candidates to become Behavior-Powered Results.

Behavior-Powered Results
Results that will improve significantly when large groups of people do Vital Behaviors consistently.

Examples of Behavior-Powered Results

Here are three examples of Behavior-Powered Results:

Improve school attendance for students in K–12. In one school district, 28% of students are chronically absent, which means they've missed 15 or more days of school for any reason. Three neighboring school districts with similar demographics have achieved between 18–21%. All the districts have similar administrative systems, personnel, and processes to address attendance.

Improve patient satisfaction. One healthcare system has an average patient satisfaction score of 3.1 out of 5, as rated via government-mandated surveys. Customers complain that they are not listened to or treated with respect. Comparable healthcare systems score on average 3.8.

Increase customer loyalty. One car dealership has only 16% of its auto buyers returning to use the service department. A competitor retains 28% of these customers in its service department. The pricing of services is about the same for both dealerships, but the customer complaints are three times as many for the first dealership.

How to Calculate How Much It Is Worth to Address Behavior Variability

In all of our years of consulting, we usually found that it's pretty easy for people to find Behavior-Powered Results. Once they become aware of the power of Vital Behaviors, they begin to see unwanted and unproductive behavior variability in many places. They can't unsee it. They also now understand how that variability adversely affects the results they need—and they want to do something about it.

Occasionally we've been asked to quantify how behavioral consistency will improve a targeted result. When that is needed, we use the conceptual measure called the Potential for Improving Performance (PIP) developed by Thomas F. Gilbert, a pioneer in Human Performance Engineering. It's a straightforward metric that compares exemplary performance to average performance on a specific dimension (e.g., quality, quantity, cost) to determine the potential for improvement. This is done by using the following formula:

$$\text{PIP} = \frac{\text{Results Achieved by Exemplary Performer}}{\text{Average of Results Achieved by Others}}$$

For example, if the best performer at an automobile dealership usually sells 20 cars a month and the average for everyone else is 4, then the PIP is 5.0. We can then calculate how much it would be worth in hard dollars if every salesperson achieved exemplary performance. Gilbert referred to this as translating the PIP into "stakes" or an economic value. That way you can determine if the cost of addressing the PIP is worth it.

Gilbert collected years of data on PIPs in a variety of industries. He derived some general guidelines on how to determine if a PIP is big enough to address:

For high-reliability industries or jobs. PIPs larger than 1.0 need to be addressed for jobs that require high precision such as airline pilots, surgeons, and nuclear plant operators. Everyone should be performing at exemplary levels!

In the general world of work. PIPs of 5.0 or more at the individual level are common and merit more attention.

For comparisons among departments, sites, or organizations. PIPs of 3.0 point toward an improvement opportunity at the management level.

For routine jobs or tasks. Even with low PIPs between 1.2 and 3.0, performance can also be significantly improved. Examples of routine job positions include bookkeeper, bank teller, housekeeper, farm worker, waitstaff, and machine operator. Routine tasks include adhering to safety procedures, completing expense reports, and debugging code.

Regardless of whether you need to quantify the potential for improvement, or you already know it exists because behavior variability is so obvious, the important thing is that you discuss these opportunities with others to get broad agreement on which Behavior-Powered Results should be top priorities to address.

Where Do You Find Behavior-Powered Results?

Look in these seven places to uncover potential Behavior-Powered Results that would get better by implementing a Vital Behavior Blueprint:

1. **Examine your organizational plans for execution risks.** Check your strategic and business plans for candidates. Look for goals that cascade to the work-unit level broadly across your organization that you are not sure will be attained, even though people have been properly trained and the right resources have been provided. Also study your organization's project portfolio.

2. **Look for inconsistent adherence.** Assess whether low adherence to work processes and procedures is negatively affecting results—even after training (and retraining!) and proper resourcing.

3. **Determine where you have low accountability for adherence.** Do you see results that are negatively impacted because leaders don't address undesired behavior variability?

4. **Identify where you see high variability in results.** If you see significant difference between the results of high and low performers, even though they both have the same resources, then the difference might be due to high behavior variability.

5. **Analyze customer complaints.** Do customer complaints point to specific results that need to be improved? Using a hotel example, are the complaints targeted more toward housekeeping, registration, or the dining room?

6. **Uncover where clear expectations are lacking.** Do you have new initiatives or work processes that require behavior change to accomplish the results? Are people clear about what they need to do differently? If not, consider elevating these results to the status of Behavior-Powered Results.

7. **Revisit results that have stalled despite other improvement efforts.** If you've tried everything to improve performance, from training to new technology, and it still hasn't worked, consider a focus on Vital Behaviors to get your organization unstuck.

Behavior-Powered Results Review

We recommend assembling a team to conduct a Behavior-Powered Results Review. The outcome of the review is a list of organizational results that are jeopardized by behavior variability. As a team, review the organizational plans and other data the team thinks will be important.

During the review, ask each team member to independently list results they think are at risk, due to real or perceived behavioral inconsistency across large groups of people. Then, have everyone together discuss the items on their lists. For each result, have the team answer the following questions:

- Is this result measured and in our business plans?
- Do many people produce this result?
- If we observed 5 employees would we see behavior variance?
- Are we at risk of not achieving this result if we let behaviors vary?

During the discussion, if the majority said "yes" to two or more of these questions for a specific results target, flag that result as a potential Behavior-Powered Result.

A word of caution: Avoid the temptation to say, "We'll just retrain everyone." We find time and again that it's the go-to solution for leaders because it's easy. The truth is, training seldom leads to sustainable behavior change. Research shows that only 10–20% of the knowledge gained in training is put into practice at work. For new behaviors to stick after training, they have to be consistently reinforced back on the job. That's where a focus on Vital Behaviors will help.

Consolidate a list of results the entire team thinks should be considered to be Behavior-Powered Results. If you feel you have too many to manage effectively, your next step will be to prioritize them.

How Do You Prioritize Behavior-Powered Results?

We've created a handy Priority Grid (Figure 10) to help the team determine where to focus first. Consider:

How high/low is the current behavior variability? (horizontal axis). Are your people consistently adhering to protocols, procedures, and work processes, just like airline pilots scrupulously follow their checklists? Or, do you see a high degree of unwanted, unproductive behavior variability leading to rework, errors, customer complaints, wasted management time, etc.?

How many/few people are producing the targeted result? (vertical axis). Plan to turn on a Vital Behavior Blueprint only when you need large groups of people, in one or more Key Performer Groups, to do things consistently.

Place each result where it best fits on the Priority Grid shown in Figure 8. (For example, if many people are responsible for producing the result, and they have high behavior variability, place it in upper left Quadrant 1.)

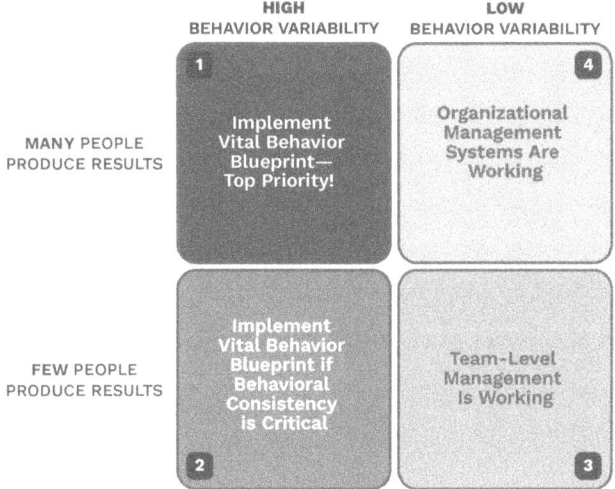

Figure 10

For the results you placed in the Quadrants 1 and 2, it means that some essential performance support is missing (clarity, feedback, barrier removal)—whether you know it or not. Let's look at the grid quadrant-by-quadrant. If you placed your results in:

Quadrant 1 (*many* people producing results, *high* behavior variability). Focus first on these results, because there is power in having many people pulling in the same direction. Build a Vital Behavior Blueprint here.

Quadrant 2 (*few* people, ***high*** variability). Focus second on these results. Build a Vital Behavior Blueprint for these results only if they are strategically important and behavior consistency is necessary, even among a small number of employees. (Example: If you depend on 10 salespeople doing the right things to bring in the money, and their results vary dramatically among them, then develop a Vital Behavior Blueprint to support those 10, and everyone else who will be added as you grow your salesforce.)

Quadrant 3 (*few* people, *low* variability). Congratulations! You are living in the best of all possible worlds. Your local team leaders so thoroughly reinforce these behaviors that you don't need to provide purposeful performance support or formal accountability using a Vital Behavior Blueprint. Your local team leaders have created a vibrant culture where "it's just how we do things here," and everyone knows it.

Quadrant 4 (*many* people, *low* variability). Congratulations again! Your current organizational management systems are working. You already have the necessary clarity, feedback, and barrier removal in place system-wide. You don't need to create a Vital Behavior Blueprint for these results.

A few of our clients have built this Behavior-Powered Results Review into their business planning process. It's completed on an annual basis to bring more alignment to their execution processes. The Vital Behaviors that support their Behavior-Powered Results get high visibility and accountability every day, leading to best-in-class results.

Avoid These Top 5 Mistakes When Selecting Behavior-Powered Results

We asked several colleagues who have facilitated Behavior-Powered Results Reviews to share their key learnings. All of them said that leaders are grateful to finally have a way to talk about the real behavior challenges inherent in implementation. As a result of doing this review, they no longer feel alone. Then they recommended that all leaders, from the top of the organization to the front line, avoid the following five mistakes to make sure they are successful.

MISTAKE #1:
Not Developing a Common Understanding of the Behavior-Powered Result

Make sure everyone understands what they are trying to achieve. A quick way to test understanding is to ask people at every level to describe any visual displays, reports, or metrics they have of the Behavior-Powered Results. This can reveal significant misalignment that you can quickly correct. The goal is to get clear about how the metrics and goals are calculated and shared with people.

MISTAKE #2:
Focusing on Too Many Results

For each Vital Behavior Blueprint, choose no more than 1 or 2 Behavior-Powered Results for all Key Performers to improve together. If you choose more than that, it gets cumbersome and muddy, making it very difficult for your busy people to focus sharply on the link between their behaviors and the Behavior-Powered Results. So, stick to 1 or 2 results, and backlog any others to consider later.

MISTAKE #3:
Picking "One-and-Done" Goals

Don't pick goals that depend on one-and-done behaviors, such as "100% of employees completed food preparation training." Experience shows this is ineffective in producing sustainable results. Instead, select goals that depend on repetitive actions that employees need to do every time. In this case, a much better goal would be, "100% of food is served at the right temperature," which shows that the training was effective.

MISTAKE #4:
Choosing a Behavior-Powered Result That is Not Yet Properly Resourced

Don't choose a goal that starts out handicapped! Do not implement a Vital Behavior Blueprint if your performance improvement effort is not yet properly resourced and structured. If people lack the tools, time, authority, skills, agreed-upon work processes, etc. to do the right things, they will be endlessly frustrated when asked to do Vital Behaviors they *can't* do. Get the resourcing in place first.

MISTAKE #5:
Choosing a Behavior-Powered Result Without Considering Its Potential Ripple Effect

Make sure you consider how performance improvement in one area might have a positive or negative ripple effect on the rest of the organization. Look for any potential negative ripple effects. For example, just because sales increases its performance by 10%, it doesn't mean manufacturing can produce 10% more. Or, when purchasing reduces costs by buying cheaper surgical gloves, it must not make it less safe for people in the operating room when they use those gloves.

Remember, all parts of your organization are interconnected! A change in one area will influence other areas, so make sure to consider both upstream and downstream effects of improving the Behavior-Powered Result you choose.

 Hospice Care Organization—STEP 1

Here is the output that Darlene and her team approved for Step 1:

Behavior-Powered Result #1. Percent of perfect care visits per month, as rated by patients' caregivers.

Behavior-Powered Result #2. Number of after-hours support calls per month made by patients/caregivers.

Figure 11 shows the start of a visual summary for this Vital Behavior Blueprint.

CASE STUDY: HOSPICE AGENCY
Vital Behavior Blueprint

Figure 11

7

STEP 2: Identify Key Performer Groups

When Key Performer Groups align around a few Vital Behaviors and do them consistently together, results soar. The second step in building your Vital Behavior Blueprint is to find those Key Performer Groups that most strongly impact the Behavior-Powered Results.

Key Performer Groups
Specific groupings of people who directly produce targeted results and are currently demonstrating lots of unwanted behavior variability that sub-optimize those results.

Examples of Key Performer Groups

Here are three examples of Key Performer Groups:

Parents, who are the key to improving school attendance. They have the greatest influence on whether kids go to school.

Healthcare providers, who are the key to improving patient satisfaction. Providers such as physicians, nurse practitioners, and physician assistants are the team leaders who have the biggest impact on patient satisfaction.

Auto service technicians, who are the key to increasing customer loyalty. The quality of their diagnostic and repair skills determines whether customers return.

To find Key Performer Groups, remember that you are seeking groups of people who need to do the same behaviors to improve results. Key Performer Groups can be clustered by various characteristics, such as:

- Everyone involved in achieving a result (examples: All team members who directly interface with customers; all facilities personnel who affect the building's cleanliness and functioning)

- Job title

- Role (in the job, work process, community, family, etc.)

- Length of employment or level of experience (new vs. long-term people, trainees vs. skilled)

- Geography

- Demographics

You can have multiple Key Performer Groups in any given behavior-powered improvement effort. For example, if you are trying to improve "student achievement for classroom performance," teachers need to be a Key Performer Group. Another (but less obvious) Key Performer Group might include both truancy officers and social workers who are responsible for attendance. (After all, students can't perform well in the classroom if they are not there.) You will need the coordinated efforts of all Key Performer Groups to achieve the mutual goal related to "student achievement in the classroom."

Where Do You Find Key Performer Groups?

Here are six ways to discover Key Performer Groups for the Behavior-Powered Results you've selected.

1. **Identify the groups most accountable for the results.** This means finding those groups that are accountable for actually producing the product or service. We're always tempted to look to the frontline first, but sometimes the Key Performer Groups lie elsewhere. Here's a striking example: In a project with a global energy company, we found the Key Performer Group to be the top 60 executives! They needed to improve their own behaviors related to making better investment decisions. Their Behavior-Powered Result was ROCE (Return On Capital Employed), a key competitive metric eyed closely by investors. The executives' behaviors were at the heart of this metric.

2. **Analyze the roles in the organizational chart.** Determine which groups are responsible for producing the Behavior-Powered Results.

3. **Identify community and family support systems.** Some Behavior-Powered Results are produced by people outside your organization. For example, community and family members might be needed to achieve your organization's public health goals. When that happens, list all the key people involved in producing the result. Group them according to role, age, or whatever parameters makes sense to create Key Performer Groups. Briefly describe their role in producing the results. Then, give this Key Performer Group a name.

4. **Examine the roles in work processes.** Try putting the process flowchart up on a wall and ask everyone to place five red dots on the behavior hotspots. Those are the process steps people don't like to

do, or don't do reliably. You will quickly see where human behavior needs some loving attention! It usually happens at decision points, handoffs, and process steps that take more effort. The next step is to ask: Who is responsible for doing these steps? This might uncover a Key Performer Group.

5. **Look for participants in project reviews.** Find those groups who meet for project reviews to see what they should be talking about and doing at each review point. For example, in the software development project we shared earlier, software team members consistently did two Vital Behaviors during project reviews: (1) "bring up barriers immediately," and (2) "track and celebrate when they are surfaced."

6. **Identify groups most affected by an organizational change.** See which part of the organization will be most impacted by the change because it will require people to do things differently. It's hard to change habits, but a Vital Behavior Blueprint will surround them with positive support.

How Do You Prioritize Key Performer Groups?

Ask the team: If we could choose only one Key Performer Group, which one would it be? Use these criteria:

- Is this group closest to the work?

- Will this group have the biggest impact because it has a large number of people?

- Will this group set in motion a chain reaction or cascade of behavior change in others, because the group is a behavior influencer?

(Example: In some regions of developing countries, mothers have the biggest impact on the nutritional choices and health outcomes for their own family and for others, so they constitute a Key Performer Group.)

- Will this group build the fastest traction?
- Does this group have high behavior variability (and what evidence do we have of that, or need to get)?

Ask the same questions for any Key Performer Groups you are considering. Then make your final selections.

Avoid These Top 4 Mistakes When Selecting Key Performer Groups

Across the decades of client projects we've conducted, these are the top mistakes we've learned to avoid when selecting Key Performer Groups.

MISTAKE #1:
Not Analyzing Whether Behavior Variability Is Really a Problem

The key here is to gather trustworthy behavioral data. This can be done by conducting direct observations, facilitating focus groups, and reviewing survey comments from customers. It can also be done through behavioral interviewing of Key Performers and their leaders. Take the time to do this! People in the potential Key Performer Groups should contribute to this data so they don't feel blamed if behavior hotspots are uncovered.

Also, there's a chance that perceived variability might not match reality. For example, if a few nurses have made medication errors, you might be tempted to set up a Vital Behavior Blueprint. Instead, gather data to see if the behavior variability is widespread. If not, handle the few individual outliers through your performance management system instead.

MISTAKE #2:
Not Targeting Where Behavior Variability Is a Problem

Is behavior variability occurring across the entire organization? Or, are results dramatically different at one site, division, or region due to behavior variability? Is variability occurring only at system bottlenecks, or everywhere across a work process? Avoid using a broad brush when defining a Key Performer Group. Instead, use a more surgical approach by pinpointing exactly where the behavior challenges are occurring.

MISTAKE #3:
Selecting Too Many Key Performer Groups

For each Vital Behavior Blueprint, choose no more than 1 to 3 Key Performer Groups, so leaders and other influencers can keep track of how to support groups in their areas. If you select more than that, it can become harder to manage. So, consider consolidating or grouping them differently to focus on the most fundamental behaviors they all share. Or, just begin with 1 to 3 groups and add more later if desired.

MISTAKE #4:
Making Leaders the Initial Key Performer Group, Rather than People Closest to the Work

It's tempting to say, "If our leaders would just hold people accountable, then we won't have to identify the Vital Behaviors for people who report to them. So let's just make leaders a Key Performer Group." This sounds good, but the problem is that leaders need to know exactly who to coach and what specific behaviors they should coach. By focusing first on the Key Performer Groups closest to the work, you give leaders the information they need to coach effectively and establish positive accountability.

 ## Hospice Care Organization—STEP 2

Here is the output that Darlene and her team approved for Step 2:

Key Performer Group #1. Nurses who lead in-home hospice care teams and have a big impact on whether the care visit is perfect overall and whether the caregiver calls 911 (implement this group immediately).

Key Performer Group #2. Chaplains, social workers, and nurse aides who impact the emotional and spiritual aspects of the perfect visit (implement this group later, if needed).

Figure 12 shows the continued building of the Vital Behavior Blueprint for nurses in Darlene's organization.

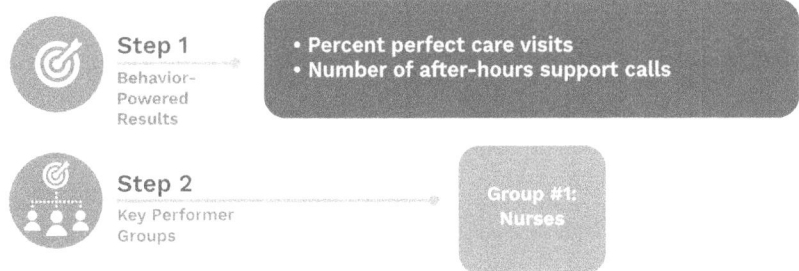

Figure 12

8

STEP 3:
Clarify Vital Behaviors

Vital Behaviors follow the 80/20 principle: 20% of our efforts produce 80% of the results we achieve. So, to transform results, you need to focus on the few Vital Behaviors that yield the highest return. The third step in building your Vital Behavior Blueprint is to make sure that the behaviors you select to embed as habits are both *clear* to Key Performers and truly *vital* to producing the Behavior-Powered Results. The output of this step will be a Vital Behavior starter set for each Key Performer Group. You will be able to implement the starter set immediately and update it as needed over time.

Vital Behaviors
The vital few mission-critical behaviors that will dramatically improve targeted results when a large group of people make them habits.

Examples of Vital Behaviors

Vital Behaviors can be relatively straightforward (like safety procedures) or extremely complex (like decision-making). They can be identified at any level of an organization. Here are three examples of Vital Behaviors:

Parents' Vital Behaviors to improve school attendance. Establish bedtime routines with their kids to improve school attendance. And track their child's attendance rates.

Healthcare providers' Vital Behaviors to improve patient satisfaction. Include patients/families in healthcare decisions that affect their care to improve the patient's follow-through on their care plan and overall patient satisfaction.

Auto service technicians' Vital Behaviors to increase customer loyalty. Discuss options and costs with car owners before repairs occur, to increase customer loyalty.

What Qualifies as a Vital Behavior?

Every Vital Behavior must meet two criteria: Clear and vital:

1. The behavior must be *clear*—

    - Who does the behavior? (Key Performer Group)

    - What behavior should they do? (observable action)

    - When should they do it? (time or step in work process)

    - Where should they do it? (physical location)

    - Why should they do it? (Behavior-Powered Results)

2. The behavior must be *vital*—

   - Necessary to achieve Behavior-Powered Result?

   - Should be done by everyone in the Key Performer Group?

   - Frequent opportunities to do the behavior?

   - Observed by others who can provide actionable feedback?

   - High behavior variability now occurring?

Here is a good example of a Clear Vital Behavior: "Direct care staff wash hands in the sink in the patient's room at the beginning of a visit to decrease hospital-acquired infections." This meets both criteria for clear and vital:

CLEAR:	
Who does it?	Direct care staff
What behavior?	Wash their hands
When?	At the beginning of a visit
Where?	In the sink in the patient room
Why do it (result)?	To decrease hospital-acquired infections

VITAL:	
Necessary to achieve Behavior-Powered Result?	Yes
Should be done by everyone?	Yes
Frequent opportunities?	Yes
Observed by others?	Yes
High behavior variability now?	Yes

Now, here is an example that is not a Clear Vital Behavior: "Direct care staff arrive to work 10 minutes before scheduled start time every shift in their hospital unit to decrease hospital-acquired infections."

	CLEAR:
Who does it?	Direct care Staff
What behavior?	Arrive at work 10 minutes before scheduled start time
When?	Every shift
Where?	In their hospital unit
Why do it (result)?	To decrease hospital-acquired infections

	VITAL:
Necessary to achieve Behavior-Powered result?	No
Should be done by everyone?	Yes
Frequent opportunities?	Yes
Observed by others?	Yes
High behavior variability now?	Yes

This behavior meets the "clear" criteria, but it's not a Clear Vital Behavior because "Arrive to work 10 minutes before scheduled start time" is not vital: It does not directly contribute to decreasing hospital-acquired infections.

Where Do You Find Clear Vital Behaviors?

As you seek Vital Behaviors for a Key Performer Group, here are seven ways to collect information (for more details, see Chapter 2):

1. Look for obvious behaviors that should be more consistent.

2. Ask the people who do the work.

3. Ask the experts.

4. Observe high and low performers.

5. Analyze your customer's journey.

6. Find behavior hot spots in your work processes.

7. Look for cornerstone behaviors that are foundational to other behaviors.

How Do You Prioritize Vital Behaviors to Create Your Starter Set?

Avoid overload! Use this process to create your Vital Behavior starter set:

1. **List all the potential Vital Behaviors you've gathered.** Capture the behaviors on sticky notes, in an Excel file, or wherever you can easily move them around and edit them.

2. **Set aside any that are not truly behavioral.** Example: "Have a good attitude." That one's no good: It's vague, there is not an action specified, you can't measure it, and people will disagree on what it means anyway.

3. **Organize the remaining behaviors.** Use one of these organizing methods:

   - If needed, create behavior categories that represent distinct responsibilities of the Key Performer Group. Example: In a fast food restaurant, Behavior Categories might be (1) teamwork, (2) food preparation, and (3) customer service. Place relevant Vital Behaviors under each category.

   - Create sequential checklists. If the Vital Behaviors must be performed sequentially, such as when blood is drawn in a clinic, group them step-by-step, rather than into general Behavior Categories.

4. **Clarify what you have.** Combine similar behaviors and rewrite unclear items until they meet the Clear Vital Behavior criteria.

5. **Create a Vital Behavior starter set and keep it short.** Please, no more than 5 to 7 behaviors! (If you absolutely must have more, then organize them by behavior categories—no more than 3 categories, with a maximum of 7 Vital Behaviors in each.)

6. **Ensure that Vital Behaviors can be measured easily.** Without measurement, you will have no way to gauge the correlation between behaviors and results. Measurement parameters to consider are frequency, quality, duration, and timeliness. For example, there are many options for measuring the behaviors of restaurant servers:

    - The number of daily specials they upsell (frequency).

    - The scores they receive on their service behaviors rated by customers (quality).

    - The average time it takes them to serve a table, start to finish (duration).

    - How many minutes it takes them to greet a customer and take their drink order once seated (timeliness).

    Easy ways to measure behavior include direct observation checklists or surveys completed as soon as possible after the Vital Behaviors occurred. Either one should be completed by Allies who have the chance to see the Key Performer in action (see the following Chapter 9, STEP 4: "Wire" Ally Feedback Loops).

If this all seems complicated, remember: Roughly right is good enough to get started! You won't know whether a behavior is truly vital until the Vital Behaviors are implemented and the results start to change. People will enjoy experimenting to see what works. They also will love having a say in dynamically updating Vital Behaviors over time as conditions change.

Avoid These Top 6 Mistakes When Selecting Vital Behaviors

Vital Behaviors are at the very core of the entire Vital Behavior Blueprint. You will want to spend sufficient time on Step 3 to make sure you have clarity and agreement about what Key Performer Groups need to do. Here are the top six mistakes to avoid so you can get alignment faster.

MISTAKE #1:
Using General Labels Instead of Specific Behavioral Descriptions

You (and everybody) tend to describe behaviors using general labels or imprecise descriptions of what someone did, like "The ride-share driver was reckless," or "The doctor was very considerate," or "The server had a good attitude." Labels like "reckless" or "good attitude" are shorthand summaries of a number of behaviors. If you want ride-share drivers to drive safely, you will need to describe the specific behaviors that make up safe driving (e.g., keep 100% of your attention on driving, be aware of other drivers, drive the speed limit or below, keep a 2-second cushion between you and the car in front of you.)

MISTAKE #2:
Describing Behaviors Too Specifically

As you learn more about writing a Clear Vital Behavior, you'll tend to swing to the other extreme and get too detailed. Our suggestions:

Keep your Vital Behavior description short. Try to keep your description to 100 characters or less (100 characters = roughly 15–25 words). This forces you to focus sharply.

Provide only enough detail needed for experienced members of a Key Performer Group. A Vital Behavior should not replace detailed policies, procedures, manuals, and protocols. Instead, they should serve as a reminder of the most Vital Behavior that has to be done. For example, on the surgical checklist, one behavior that needs to occur at the end of every surgery is: "Nurse verbally confirms with the team that the counts are correct for instruments, sponges, and needles." This behavior is vital for ensuring the team doesn't leave anything inside the patient that shouldn't be there! At first blush, this behavior seems so simple. Yet there is a reason why, as the American Society of Anesthesiologists reports, about a dozen sponges and other surgical instruments are left inside patients' bodies every day, resulting in 4,500–6,000 cases per year in the U.S. This simple step of having the team confirm the count is often missed. That's why it's important to keep the Vital Behavior at the level of detail that can be understood and adhered to by typical experienced employees. (If less-experienced members of the surgical team want more detail about how to manage these items during surgery to make sure they aren't left in patients, etc., they can visit procedures, protocols, manuals, and job aids to learn how to do the Vital Behavior.)

MISTAKE #3:
Selecting Behaviors Based on What Not to Do

Negatives don't work well with people. So, don't focus on what a Key Performer Group should not do, like "Registration personnel should not keep patients guessing about when they'll see the doctor." Instead, focus on what they need to do: "Registration personnel are to inform patients every 15 minutes of progress and delays while in the waiting room."

MISTAKE #4:
Saying "These Vital Behaviors Are Final" to Key Performers

That can really put them off, like dictating to them! This is why we recommend creating a starter set of Vital Behaviors that is good enough to get going. From there, the data will tell you if you are focused on the right behaviors or need to adjust. People don't like to feel that they are locked into doing Vital Behaviors forever—especially if the behaviors are not yet proven to be necessary toward producing the Behavior-Powered Results reliably.

MISTAKE #5:
Not Letting Key Performers Tailor the Vital Behaviors

Key Performers need to feel like they own the Vital Behaviors. They want the freedom to make them fit better with their local practices, terms, tools, etc. For example, when we worked with a global airline to improve the inflight experience for frequent flyers, one of the Vital Behaviors was to "greet each frequent flyer upon boarding by smiling, making eye contact, and thanking them by name for choosing the airline." The problem: In some parts of the world, making eye contact is considered disrespectful, so Key Performers were encouraged to tailor that Vital Behavior to better fit their local customs and cultures.

MISTAKE #6:
Forgetting to Find the "Want To" for the Vital Behaviors

Even when people are actively engaged in identifying Vital Behaviors, there always comes that emotional moment when they think, "Ugh, do I really have to do this?" Some people can bust through that moment to find the personal rewards for doing the new behaviors. Others need more convincing about why these behaviors are so critical. Most times it's not enough to say, "If you do these behaviors, we will improve these organizational results." Instead, the behaviors must connect at an emotional level for people. They must be personally rewarding, not just for the organization.

Here's a great story about the importance of "want to": Co-author Julie Smith helped a telecom's customer call center transition from being a customer service center to becoming a sales/service center. When employees heard the plan, they went ballistic at the idea of adding selling to their roles. Even though a high-engagement approach was used to identify and test new Vital Behaviors for sales, 80% of service representatives did not want to change their role. They said things like, "If I wanted to be a pushy salesperson, I would have started in sales," and "Customers don't want us selling to them when they are already angry about service issues."

So Julie and her team used four powerful ways to find the "want to" for the customer service reps (these can work for your effort too!):

1. **Find a way for the Vital Behaviors to complement the Key Performers' current identity.** Call center personnel thought of themselves as problem-solvers who were on the customer's side. That was their deeply ingrained identity. They didn't want to upsell products that they thought customers wouldn't want or need. So, we made it okay to talk with the customer and down sell them to a more appropriate suite of services if that would better meet the customer's needs. This simple twist overcame almost all of the resistance. Customers loved it, and ironically, sales increased as the customer and call center rep spent time getting to know the customer's true needs.

2. **Share customer success stories broadly.** Key influencers among the center reps were asked to share early success stories of how they delighted customers by focusing on both service and sales. For example, for the customer with young children, reps were able to offer more cost-effective family packages that included safety features. Customers loved it! These stories helped everyone see why the transition was important to customers.

3. **Share positive stories of the internal ripple effect.** The company's in-home installers found their lives vastly improved too. The notes captured by the call center reps helped them better understand a customer's total needs, allowing installers to better service the customer when they were on-site. Their in-home stories were captured and shared with the call center reps, which made the reps want to continue doing the Vital Behaviors.

4. **Expose Key Performers to other organizations doing the same thing.** We scheduled trips to other call centers that had made the switch to combining sales and service. It was an eye-opener for the reps to learn why others were making this change: Busy customers were now demanding a one-call resolution to their issues. So, it was not unreasonable for their company to ask call center reps to focus on sales. It was where the industry was headed.

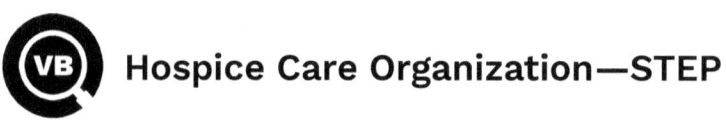

Hospice Care Organization—STEP 3

Figure 13 continues building Darlene's Vital Behavior Blueprint, showing the output Darlene and her team approved for Step 3.

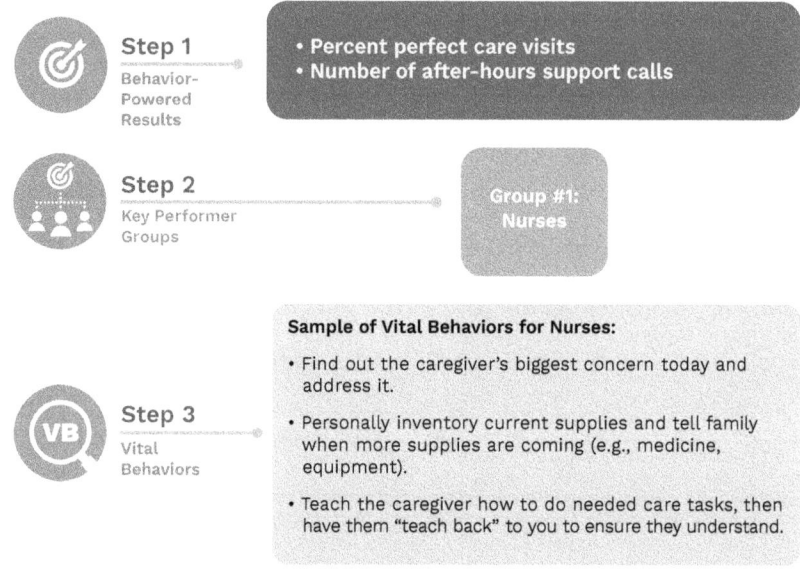

Figure 13

9

STEP 4:
"Wire" Ally Feedback Loops

How can a Key Performer—or anyone—improve if no one tells them how they're doing? This is why Ally Feedback Loops are critical. They help Allies provide valuable insights to Key Performers that clarify expectations, inspire individual behavior change, improve your organization's products and services, and enhance everyone's overall experience. When it's all said and done, feedback is the lifeblood of Ally Networks—they cannot thrive without the steady flow of feedback.

Step 4 helps your organization wire those feedback loops by establishing feedback pathways between Allies and Key Performers that are powerful and virtually realtime.

Ally Feedback Loops

Provide behavior-changing information from Allies to Key Performers about whether Vital Behaviors and associated work outputs are meeting expectations and producing the targeted results everyone wants.

What Are Ally Feedback Loops?

Remember, Gallup reports only 30% of employees have received actionable feedback in the last seven days. In the hundreds of organizations we've consulted with through the years, we've always found that feedback is the low-hanging fruit for achieving an immediate, positive effect on performance and employee morale. It doesn't take a lot of effort, and it has a big impact. Never underestimate the power of feedback! Here are three examples of Ally Feedback Loops:

School truancy officers (as Allies) help parents (Key Performers) track attendance. Truancy Officers send text messages daily to parents regarding whether their kids are present, absent, or late.

Patients (as Allies) help healthcare providers (Key Performers) improve care delivery. While waiting to be discharged, patients provide feedback on how included they felt in the development of their care plan and the likelihood they will carry it out.

Customers (as Allies) provide auto service technicians (Key Performers) with feedback on service/repairs. Customer satisfaction is tracked by car and by the individuals who worked on it. Front-counter staff track the cars that were serviced right the first time and those that were brought back for rework.

Effective Ally Feedback

Effective Ally Feedback is:

- Timely, so adjustments can be made promptly.

- Actionable, so people know what they should or should not do.

- Balanced, by the "Magic 5:1 Feedback Ratio" between positive and constructive feedback (for example: 5 "Great jobs!" to 1 "Keep trying").

- Bidirectional, to achieve mutual understanding.

- Behavior-changing, until results are achieved.

- Rewarding for the giver, because they see whether their feedback had a positive impact.

Where Do You Find Ally Groups to Provide Feedback?

Effective Ally Feedback Loops are the most common missing piece in performance improvement initiatives. That means that you might have to construct new feedback loops from the ground up.

You start by looking for groups of Allies who can provide behavior-changing, timely feedback to the Key Performers. They can do this because they can observe Key Performers in action and assess whether the Vital Behaviors and work outputs meet expectations.

Here are four ways to find Ally Groups who can provide meaningful feedback to Key Performers:

1. **Prioritize customer and other stakeholder groups.** Which internal/external customers and other stakeholders want to make sure their expectations and feedback are heard and acted on? If they have a stake in the game, they will be more willing to serve as Allies.

2. **Identify leader groups.** Which leader groups can provide ongoing, high-quality performance coaching through 1:1 coaching conversations, team huddles, and regular management meetings?

3. **Analyze team member groupings.** Can all team members provide meaningful feedback to individual peers? Would sub-groups of peers be a better choice? Peer feedback gives team members a way to achieve realtime alignment on performance expectations, get and give meaningful feedback to each other, proactively remove barriers together, and align daily Vital Behaviors to achieve results.

4. **Consider self-feedback.** Self-feedback should always be used in tandem with feedback from one or more of the Ally Groups discussed above. It provides individuals a way to assess how they did and compare it to the feedback they received from others. It's a gut check on extremes: Whether they are being too hard on themselves, or back-patting themselves too much. It helps them see where they need help and which Vital Behaviors they are doing well and could help others do well, too.

Create a list of all potential Ally Groups that can provide meaningful, timely feedback to Key Performers. Feel free to develop sub-groups of each Ally Group, if needed. Here's an example of additional sub-groups:

Customer Feedback Loops	Leader Feedback Loops	Team Feedback Loops
• Selected internal customers • Selected external customers	• Team leads • Supervisors • Functional experts	• A sub-group of the team • All team members

There Can Be Multiple Ally Groups if One Key Performer Group

Sometimes it works best for a Key Performer Group to get support from several different Ally Groups. They often find it beneficial to get balanced feedback from multiple perspectives. A remarkable example of Ally Feedback Loops in action comes from Iceland. For years, the island nation had among the worst records in Europe for teenage substance abuse. So, the government took a community-based approach country-wide to bring about dramatic change among the Key Performer Group, youth aged 13 and up.

Multiple Ally Groups helped young people dramatically decrease their substance abuse (smoking, drinking, illegal drug use, etc.):

Parent Ally Group. Parents set up night patrols to prompt kids to get off the streets and go home. They called each other to make sure they knew where their kids were at all times in the evenings, and kids knew these calls were being made and parents were supporting each other. Parents also made a point of being home at 5:00 to spend evenings with their kids.

Schools Ally Group. Schools agreed to keep their facilities open evenings and weekends to provide alternative, healthy activities for youth. Parents could call any time to check whether their kids were there.

Community Governance Ally Group. These groups agreed to fund, promote, and monitor the success of the program at the community level. For example, they funded leisure-time activities, even providing pre-paid memberships for kids' afterschool activities.

An annual nationwide survey measured key substance abuse indicators. The results were widely publicized and became part of a giant feedback loop to Iceland's youth and all their Allies.

These multi-pronged feedback loops connecting youth and their Allies produced stupendous results. During baseline, 48% of youth abused substances. Five years later, only 5% did so. These low rates have been maintained over two decades. The notorious heavy-drinking culture of

Iceland's youth has fundamentally changed to a culture of health and moderation, or even abstinence!

How Do You Prioritize Ally Groups to Provide Feedback?

Once you've identified all potential Ally Groups, ask: "If we could choose only one group to provide behavior-changing feedback to the Key Performers, which one would it be? And why?" Use these questions:

- **Which Ally Group is most important to Key Performers?** Who do they respect? Who do they want to make sure is happy with how they are handling things? Make sure to ask Key Performers their opinions.

- **Can this Ally Group directly observe Vital Behaviors in action or monitor work output?** Are they naturally positioned to see Key Performers in action or to monitor the quality of the service or products they produce?

- **Can this Ally Group provide timely feedback?** Can they provide feedback immediately after the Key Performer does the Vital Behavior, or at least within 24 hours?

- **Can this Ally Group be motivated to provide feedback to Key Performers when asked?** Will they be willing to provide feedback regularly, not just when they are disgruntled with the product or service?

Ask the same questions for any additional groups. Remember, never select just the Self Feedback Loop. It must be supplemented with feedback from other Ally Groups.

Now, consider which Ally Groups are "must have" versus "nice to have" for feedback. Think about energizing the must-have feedback loops first, then bringing up the nice-to-have loops later.

How Do You Activate Ally Feedback Loops?

First, find the natural point in the work process where Allies can provide feedback on Vital Behaviors. Then, craft a way to gather data from the Allies (one way is to use Vital Behavior spot checks described in Chapter 3; another is to use surveys that ask about specific behaviors). Finally, determine when those data will be made available to individual Key Performers and their teams, including when and how they will review it.

It's easier to set up these Ally Feedback Loops than you might think! And behavior will begin to change even before they are activated, because now 100% of people will know what is expected of them (instead of the typical 30%).

You will begin to create a feedback-rich culture by focusing first on Vital Behaviors that everyone has agreed to. This simple focus makes it easier for people to give and receive feedback. As they become more skilled and confident in providing non-blaming, behavior-based feedback, they will give and seek feedback for things other than the Vital Behaviors. Developmental feedback will become easier, as will performance reviews.

Avoid These Top 4 Mistakes When Creating Ally Feedback Loops

You might have to experiment with arranging feedback loops that actually produce behavior change at the individual level. Here are the top four mistakes to avoid as you explore what works.

MISTAKE #1:
Not Providing Behaviorally-Specific Feedback

The items on most feedback surveys are too general to be helpful. Example: If you were a physician and received low scores for "My doctor respected my privacy," would it tell you what to do differently? Likely not. But if the survey item were more behavioral: "My doctor asked if I wanted to speak privately about my health," a "no" answer would tell you exactly what to do to improve. By identifying Vital Behaviors, you can make survey questions very targeted.

MISTAKE #2:
Not Providing Individualized Feedback

On some surveys, it's not clear whose performance is being rated. Example: If you are a salesperson at an auto dealership and you get a low score for "The sales team communicated my credit rating in a professional manner," you might think that it was the back-office people who mishandled these discussions, not you. Instead, raters need to know the specific person they are rating (it's helpful if the survey includes a picture of the individual being rated).

MISTAKE #3:
Not Providing Timely Feedback

Feedback needs to be very prompt. It should be provided within 24 hours after the behavior occurred for it to be effective. Most people have difficulty remembering the specifics of what happened, so long delays make it hard for them to process the event and learn from it.

MISTAKE #4:
Not Considering "What's In It For Me" (WIIFM) for the Feedback Providers

Survey completion rates are typically below 20%, and they are completed mostly by two distinct groups: People who are either highly upset or highly satisfied. So, think through the WIIFMs for the feedback providers. The number one reason people don't give feedback is, "It won't make a difference anyway." So, consider sending them an automated note announcing changes you've made, based on feedback received this month. Or, consider a freebie incentive you might offer to feedback providers when they complete a survey (parking pass, a free coffee, etc.).

Hospice Care Organization—STEP 4

Here is the output that Darlene and her team approved for Step 4:

Ally Feedback Loop #1. Before each visit, the patient's caregivers will complete a short expectation pulse check that communicates their top care needs for that visit. After the visit, caregivers will complete a short pulse check to say whether their top needs were met, plus rate two randomly sampled Vital Behaviors of the nurse.

Ally Feedback Loop #2. Case managers will call five caregivers per week to check whether nurses are doing all the Vital Behaviors.

Figure 14 shows the continued building of Darlene's Vital Behavior Blueprint.

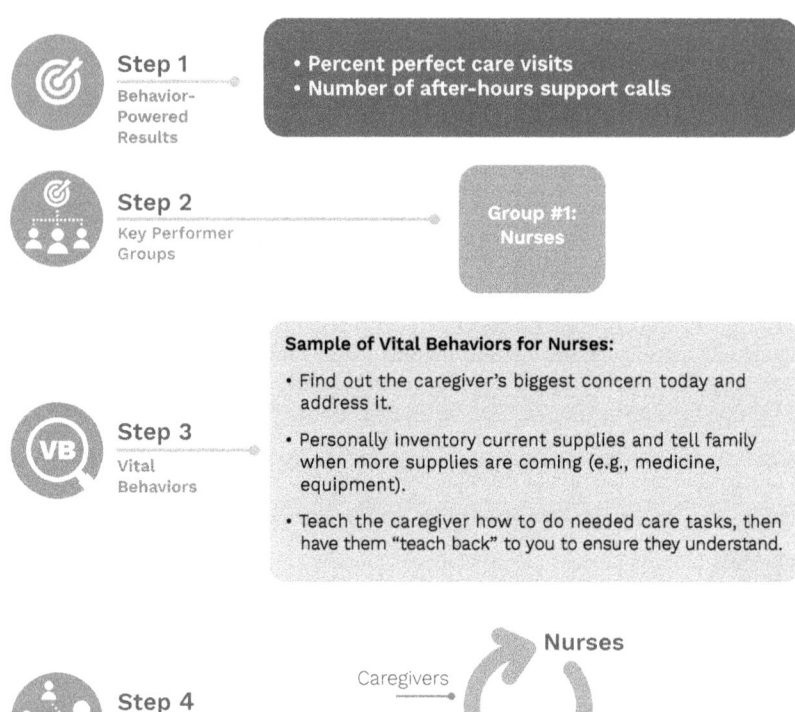

Figure 14

10

STEP 5: Build Habits Using 3 Pillars

The final step in building your Vital Behavior Blueprint is to create an environment where Vital Behaviors can thrive, free from barriers and rich in support. Sustainable habits are the result of a supportive system, not mere personal willpower. This supportive system is built on 3 Pillars: (1) Clear Expectations, (2) Actionable Feedback, and (3) Barrier Removal.

What Are the 3 Pillars Needed to Build Habits?

3 Pillars
Ongoing behavior-changing support that gives Key Performers (1) Clear Expectations, (2) Actionable Feedback, and (3) Barrier Removal so they can do Vital Behaviors to get results.

During execution, Allies help ensure that the 3 Pillars (Figure 15) are provided to all Key Performers. This support is ongoing, at least until new habits reach a high level of habit strength.

THE 3 PILLARS FOR BUILDING GOOD HABITS

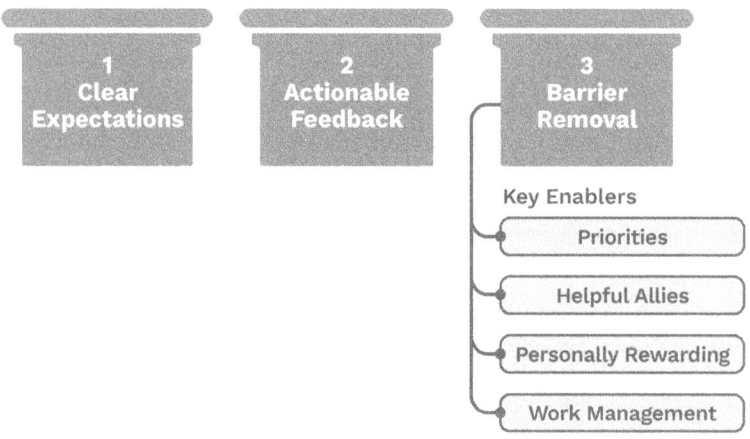

Figure 15

Pillar 1: Clear Expectations. Is every Key Performer clear on (1) the results they need to achieve, (2) what they need to do to achieve those results (especially the Vital Behaviors), and (3) the standards their work products and services need to meet (like timeliness, durability, availability, performance)?

Pillar 2: Actionable Feedback. Are individual Key Performers getting frequent, personalized feedback (at least weekly)? Is the feedback meaningful and helpful? Is it resulting in desired behavior change?

Pillar 3: Barrier Removal. Is the environment set up to support and sustain new behaviors? Or, are barriers in the way that create friction for the Key Performers, making it difficult to do the right things?

We bucket barriers into four categories that need to be turned into key enablers:

Priorities. Are Key Performers clear about where the Behavior-Powered Results fit relative to their other responsibilities? Are they sure that leaders are aligned about these priorities?

Helpful Allies. Is the work environment one where Key Performers are surrounded by positive people who support them in doing the Vital Behaviors?

Personally Rewarding. Do Key Performers see the benefits to themselves for doing the Vital Behaviors? Do they get joy out of helping the organization and other team members achieve the results? Do they feel that their managers and human resource systems will reward people fairly?

Work Management. Do work management systems help Key Performers achieve the results? (Work management systems include tools, training, work schedules and staffing, work processes, decision authority, and speedy barrier removal.)

If the answer is "no" to any of the questions above, then barriers exist that need to be removed.

Recall the example where schools were trying to improve attendance rates (the Behavior-Powered Result). They decided that parents were the Key Performer Group that most impacted attendance rates. The Vital Behaviors the parents agreed to were (1) establish a bedtime routine with their kids, and (2) regularly review their child's attendance reports. Here are examples of how the 3 Pillars were used to support these parents.

Clear Expectations. Parents needed additional tips on how to set up bedtime routines for children of different ages, because bedtime routines for teens are different from those for grade-schoolers.

Actionable Feedback. Parents wanted the schools to provide more feedback than just daily text messages about their kids' attendance. They asked for a monthly summary that showed how their kids compared to others. They also wanted the school to share research about the life consequences of good and poor attendance that they could discuss with their kids.

Barrier Removal. In a chat room that parents set up to support each other, it was discovered that some kids did not have beds, so a community group was formed to build beds and supply the bedding.

Where Do You Find Opportunities to Strengthen the 3 Pillars?

1. **Conduct a 3 Pillars Pulse Check.** Make sure Key Performers and their leaders have multiple opportunities to report if they are getting the execution support they need. Using the questions below, regularly gather data during team huddles, 1:1 conversations, and ongoing management meetings. Or, you can create an online pulse check to gather data anonymously to assess how it's going at key points. Consider conducting a pulse check after initially communicating Vital Behaviors to establish a baseline, and another six months later when you should see improvements.

   ### 3 Pillars Pulse Check for Key Performers

   - Has your leader set **clear expectations** about the Vital Behaviors and work outputs expected of you to achieve the targeted result?

   - Do you get **actionable feedback** from your leader, at least weekly, about how well you are doing on the Vital Behaviors and work outputs?

- Is **barrier removal** happening quickly with the help of your leaders and Allies so you have everything you need to perform Vital Behaviors and produce required work outputs?

- Does your leader prompt you to help others form good habits?

3 Pillars Pulse Check for Leaders

- Do you set **clear expectations** with your employees about the Vital Behaviors and work outputs needed to achieve the targeted result?

- Do you provide **actionable feedback** to each employee at least weekly about how well they are doing on the Vital Behaviors and work outputs?

- Do you ensure quick **barrier removal** so your employees have everything they need to perform Vital Behaviors and produce work outputs?

- Do you prompt your employees to help others form good habits?

- Which CORE Vital Behaviors for Leaders do you feel confident providing to your employees to help them achieve the Vital Behaviors and work output?

    - **C**larify expectations of Vital Behaviors and work outputs.

    - **O**bserve and monitor Vital Behaviors and work outputs.

    - **R**einforce (or redirect) Vital Behaviors using actionable feedback.

    - **E**liminate barriers to Vital Behaviors and work outputs.

2. **Reinforce surfacing problems.** When someone raises a problem area, that's a desired behavior. Reinforce it with, "Thank you for bringing that up! Help me understand what happens from your point of view." First make sure they feel heard, then help them convert the problem into an improvement opportunity.

How Do You Prioritize Improvement Opportunities to Strengthen the 3 Pillars?

Once you've compiled a list of potential improvement opportunities, determine which ones should be prioritized and tracked on a visible 3 Pillars Scorecard. Ask:

- Which ones do we need to keep an eye on?

- Where can we get quick wins for which people can take credit and celebrate?

A visible scorecard powerfully demonstrates to everyone that improvement opportunities are being tracked and addressed. The goal is to help people quickly see which opportunities exist and what is being done about them. We suggest a format for the scorecard below, but you will need to develop what works best for your organization or project.

3 Pillars Scorecard

Improvement Opportunities	Easy*	Difficult**	Responsible Person	Resolved When?

*__Easy__—Blocking immediate work, can be fixed quickly.
**__Difficult__—Not blocking immediate work, difficult to fix, will become a huge issue over time if not addressed.

Figure 16 presents an easy way to display measurable progress on strengthening the 3 Pillars. If people are addressing improvement opportunities as soon as they arise, the active opportunities being managed should go down over time, especially those that are difficult to fix. You can use this simple bar graph to track and celebrate progress.

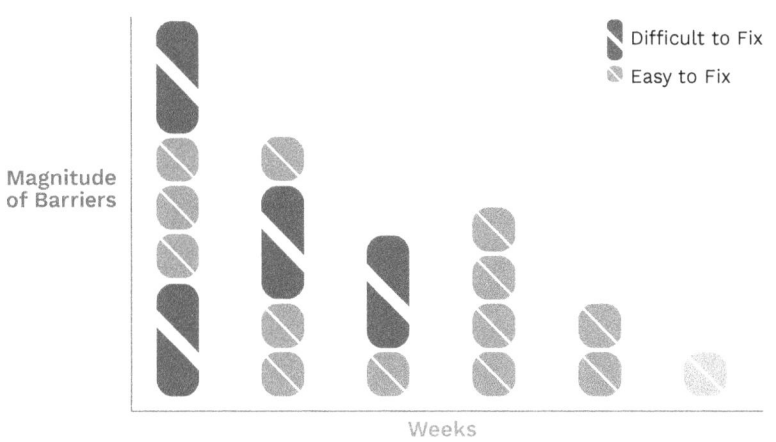

Figure 16

How often should you update your 3 Pillars Scorecard? For a 3-month project, you might need daily or weekly updates. For an ongoing, more predictable operation, twice-monthly updates might be enough. The point is to update your 3 Pillars Scorecard frequently enough to make informed decisions about resourcing improvement efforts.

A good scorecard process builds trust, opening the lines of communication across your Vital Behavior Blueprint. It also gives everyone more opportunities to help each other.

Avoid These Top 4 Mistakes When Strengthening the 3 Pillars

Step 5 is where leadership is critical. People need to know that leaders are doing everything possible to remove barriers that hamper their doing the right things. Demonstrate your commitment to the Vital Behavior Blueprint by avoiding these top four mistakes:

MISTAKE #1:
Not Encouraging People to Surface Problems ASAP

People tend to wait, thinking they can solve the problem themselves. This only causes problems later, leading to costly delays and frustration for everyone. Make sure everyone knows that "surfacing problems ASAP" is important in your culture.

MISTAKE #2:
Not Addressing Problems with Urgency

Don't let improvement opportunities sit forever! Address them promptly, no excuses. Or, talk through why they cannot be addressed right now. Discuss alternative solutions. Decide what the team can do now, versus what needs to be escalated. If an opportunity can't be addressed, take it off your list. But never pretend that a problem someone raised doesn't exist!

MISTAKE #3:
Not Having the Right Person Address the Problems

Why are some people able to move heaven and earth to get problems addressed? It's because they won't take no for an answer. They use their Ally Networks to get problems solved. They show data to illustrate how big the problem is, and the risks associated with not solving it. They involve the big guns if they have to.

If someone sits on a problem for more than two weeks with no progress, see if another person can take it over. Remember, everyone can be involved in addressing improvement opportunities, not just leaders. Use your influencing skills to engage Allies in being part of the solution—not a victim of the problem.

MISTAKE #4:
Not Being Transparent About the 3 Pillars Scorecard

Nothing upsets people more than not knowing what is happening with the scorecard, especially regarding problems they raised themselves. Keep the scorecard updated and highly visible. Communicate progress and delays so people feel confident that problems are being addressed.

 ## Hospice Care Organization—STEP 5

Here are examples of improvement opportunities that surfaced during planning and execution of the Vital Behaviors.

Improvement Opportunity #1. During planning, the project team found out that nurses are afraid to count the supply of narcotics every time because they might discover that a family member or someone is stealing them, and they don't want to deal with it.

- **Improvement Plan**—The family will watch a short video to understand their role in managing narcotics for the patient, and the legal consequences of mismanagement for everyone involved. The experience pulse check completed by patients or family will include a question asking whether the nurse counted the narcotics each visit.

Improvement Opportunity #2. During execution, nurses aren't getting actionable feedback, because caregivers are completing the expectation and experience pulse checks for only 44% of the visits.

- **Improvement Plan**—A backup call center will ensure caregivers complete these pulse checks.

Figure 17 shows the completed template for Darlene's Vital Behavior Blueprint.

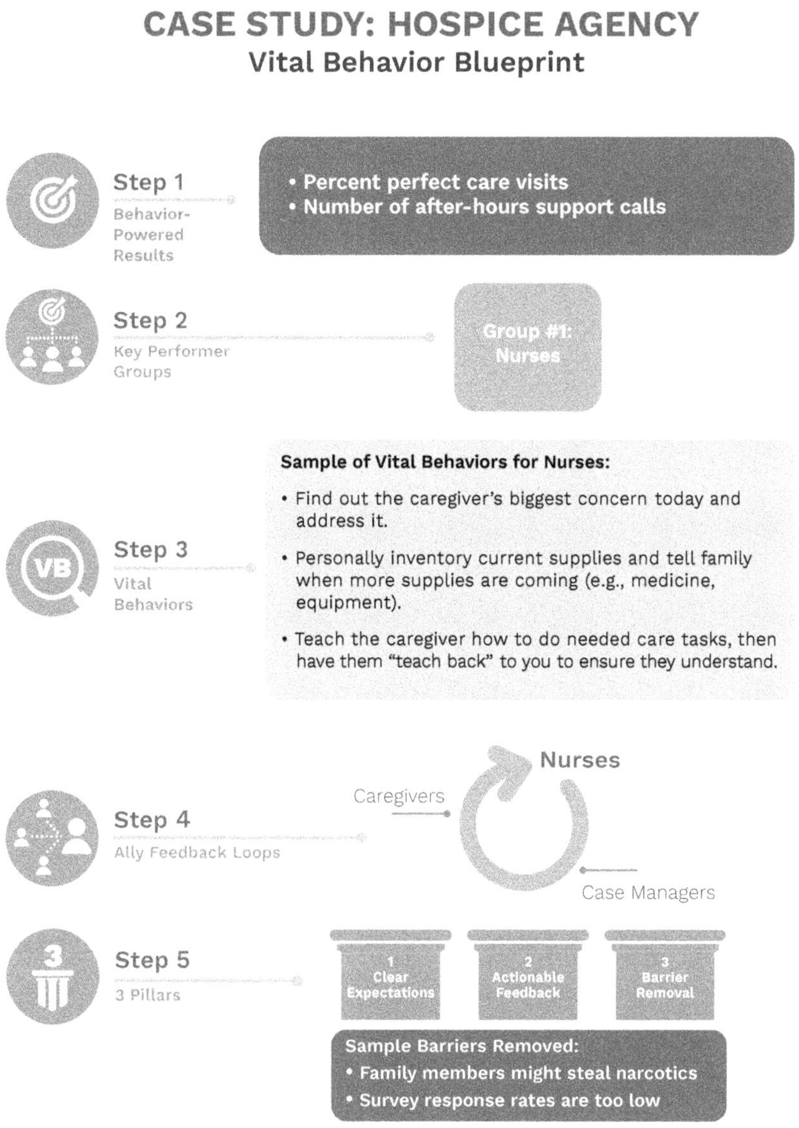

CASE STUDY: HOSPICE AGENCY
Vital Behavior Blueprint

Step 1 — Behavior-Powered Results
- Percent perfect care visits
- Number of after-hours support calls

Step 2 — Key Performer Groups

Group #1: Nurses

Step 3 — Vital Behaviors

Sample of Vital Behaviors for Nurses:
- Find out the caregiver's biggest concern today and address it.
- Personally inventory current supplies and tell family when more supplies are coming (e.g., medicine, equipment).
- Teach the caregiver how to do needed care tasks, then have them "teach back" to you to ensure they understand.

Step 4 — Ally Feedback Loops

Caregivers → Nurses ← Case Managers

Step 5 — 3 Pillars

1. Clear Expectations
2. Actionable Feedback
3. Barrier Removal

Sample Barriers Removed:
- Family members might steal narcotics
- Survey response rates are too low

Figure 17

VITAL BEHAVIOR SUCCESS STORIES

Tales from the Trenches

These true stories and insights come from organizations that used the Vital Behavior Blueprint to achieve unprecedented results. We promise that you will get many ideas to implement immediately in your organization!

Some leaders in these stories learned the Vital Behavior-powered approach directly from the authors, while others discovered it independently. Regardless, we tell their stories using the 5 Steps to show how they achieved such success.

These leaders chose to remain anonymous, as their organizations want to protect their competitive advantage. They hope that by sharing their candid experience, you will see how focusing on Vital Behaviors can supercharge your results and transform your culture.

For a growing list of success stories across a variety of performance improvement opportunities (public health, education, businesses large and small), please visit our website at **www.vitalbehaviorblueprint.com**.

11

In-Home Repair Techs Grow Their Business by Respecting Customers in a Whole New Way

In-Home ApplianceTech

The Vital Behaviors of in-home service technicians sharply increased customer satisfaction and Likelihood to Recommend for a retail chain's appliance repair service.

Seeking Ways to Grow In-Home ApplianceTech

In-Home ApplianceTech, a division of a national retail chain, had been around for decades, performing millions of in-home repairs annually. They were a middle-of-the-pack appliance-fixer, well-known and respected, but stagnating. Leadership was looking for ways to grow the division.

To grow, they had to do something different to increase their customer base. Marketing efforts were just not breaking through. The retail chain had its own house brand of appliances, but most customers were unaware that they serviced all brands of appliances, not just their own. Clearly there was plenty of room to grow market share, if they could just find the right key.

Marcus Benson (not his real name) was In-Home's Learning & Development Director and internal-workplace behavior consultant. He recalls,

"We were a multibillion-dollar division and accounted for about 7% of the total company revenue. We had around 8,000 Techs and 450 Managers nationwide providing in-home appliance services—delivery, installation, and repair. Though impressive, we knew we could do even better."

What was needed to grow? Marcus explains,

"Our customer satisfaction surveys showed that half the people who chose In-Home ApplianceTech did so because a friend or a family member had recommended them. That told us we could expand business by using family and friends as our 'advocates' to gain new customers.

"So, the next question was, why had some of our customers sent friends and family to us? And why had others *not* recommended us? To discover why, we got a vendor to provide an objective evaluation of where we stood on the Net Promoter Score®. NPS® is a well-known measure of customer loyalty. Because so many companies capture their NPS, we could use it to see where we ranked against our competitors."

Getting the Facts on Customer Satisfaction

Marcus explains how In-Home ApplianceTech measured its Net Promoter Score (NPS):

"To determine our NPS, the vendor asked our customers to rate us 1 to 10 on this statement: *I would recommend In-Home ApplianceTech to friends or family.* People who rated us 9 or 10 were our Promoters ("You should call In-Home ApplianceTech!"). People who rated us 0 to 6 were our Detractors (they would tell family and friends, "Stay away from them!"). People rating us 7 or 8 were "Passives." (See Figure 18 for a description of how to calculate NPS.)

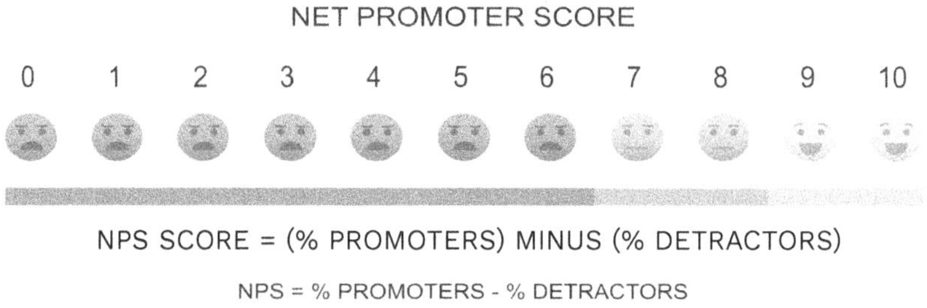

NET PROMOTER SCORE

0 1 2 3 4 5 6 7 8 9 10

NPS SCORE = (% PROMOTERS) MINUS (% DETRACTORS)

NPS = % PROMOTERS - % DETRACTORS

Figure 18

"Obviously, we wanted to maximize our Promoters. The higher our NPS Score, the better, because it predicts market share and revenue growth.

"Unfortunately, we found that our NPS ranked below the midpoint of our competition.

"So, our vendor asked our customers an additional question: *Why did you give us that number rating*? What were we doing that earned us a lower rating? When our customers rated us 9 or 10, what were we doing that made them our advocate?"

Research found, as expected, that part of the difference between high and low ratings was due to operational effectiveness: Was the service scheduled promptly? Did the technician show up on time? Did they have all the parts they needed? Did they fix your appliance correctly the first time, and quickly?

But there also was a big surprise: 80% of the difference between high and low ratings was behavioral, for example, "showing customers respect."

So leaders realized the way to grow was not through marketing, technology, or process improvement—all of these were important of course, but not the real key to growth. They saw that the key was word-of-mouth recommendations, driven by the behaviors of their own service techs.

After all, the service techs were in people's homes every day, doing more than repairs: They were the face of the company. They left powerful impressions of competence and friendliness on customers. How they behaved made all the difference, and led customers to recommend In-Home ApplianceTech to their friends.

Building a Vital Behavior Blueprint for Success

In the upcoming pages you'll discover the inspiring story of how In-Home ApplianceTech achieved remarkable growth by identifying and supercharging the Vital Behaviors of service technicians. Under Marcus's leadership, they turned the fuzzy concept of "respect" into concrete actions that customers wanted, and thousands of service techs demonstrated every day. By using the 5 Steps to build a Vital Behavior Blueprint, the In-Home ApplianceTech Division was able to deliver an entirely new service brand that created loyal customers.

Step 1: Prioritize Behavior-Powered Results *Will the Behaviors of Our People Improve Net Promoter Scores?*

Marcus notes that the business target quickly became apparent:

"The best way to increase overall growth was to improve our Net Promoter Score. Of course, we still needed to improve operational metrics, like scheduling services faster or getting repairs right the first time. These would always be critical—but they weren't the key to growing the In-Home ApplianceTech Division.

"We needed to improve our customer satisfaction ratings, based on how service technicians treated our customers in their homes. We could only do that by changing our technicians' behavior. They needed to focus on showing the customer respect, in addition to completing repairs. If we could do that in a smart way, we would create more loyal customers and increase our competitive positioning in the marketplace."

The leadership team saw a presentation of these findings and said,

"OK, so we need customer service training! There's plenty to choose from off-the-shelf. Let's get it done!"

But Marcus saw a big red flag about retraining everyone in customer service skills:

"I knew that throwing techs into some training class would achieve nothing. All my experience taught me that training might get the desired behaviors started, but it couldn't sustain them over the long haul. I also worried that off-the-shelf customer service training might miss the mark for what our customers really wanted.

"So I told the leadership team, 'Look, I need to actually see what our techs are doing in people's homes. I need to go on service calls with the techs, to see them in action, before we jump into customer service training. Because if we don't fully understand this, we might not teach our people the right skills to improve the customer relationship.'"

Step 2: Identify Key Performer Groups
Whose Behaviors Will Most Improve Net Promoter Scores?

There were three groups of employees who impacted Net Promoter Scores—delivery people, installers, and service techs. Marcus and his team decided to focus on the service techs (the repair people). They were 80% of the workforce, with more and longer customer interactions, so they had the biggest impact on the customer.

The next step for Marcus and his team was to assess the level of behavior variability among the techs. He partnered with a district general manager (GM) to observe 10% of both the top- and bottom-performing techs in the field. Since technicians were accustomed to manager ridealongs, they were comfortable with Marcus and the GM joining them on the job.

What We Saw Techs Doing in the Warehouses

Marcus notes,

"We began where service techs started their morning: The parts warehouse, where they loaded their trucks for the day. Right away, we spotted one thing that lower performers were not doing: "Review my service orders for today's scheduled repairs to make sure I have all the correct parts I need on my truck." These lower performers sometimes had to make an extra trip back to the warehouse for a part, because they had not checked their service orders. That not only cost time and money, but irritated the customer, leading to a lower rating.

"By contrast, the top performers checked their service orders before they left so they had everything they needed. This was what we call a Vital Behavior for service technicians: "Check my service orders and match it with the parts in my truck."

"This seemed obvious, but it proved my point: We didn't know about this behavior problem until we actually observed the high and low performers. Off-the-shelf customer service training would never have caught that!"

What We Saw Techs Doing In-Home

Then Marcus and the district GM went in-home to observe service techs—both high performers and low performers.

"The differences we saw were stark. The top performers truly were courteous and respectful. They kept their customers updated on whether they would arrive on time or be delayed. When they arrived, they took time to understand their customer's concerns, beyond what was written on the job order. They explained what they were doing, listened to the customer, and answered questions.

"And they treated the customer's house like they would treat their own. Customers didn't want them to track in mud, gouge walls, or spill stuff. They wanted them to leave their house as clean as they found it. It all makes sense when you think about it.

"These high-performing techs also noticed whether the customer had appliance brands other than their own. They would mention that we could repair those brands too, and told the customer they could get a service plan covering all of their appliances from one trusted source— In-Home ApplianceTech.

"Think of the power of having thousands of technicians in tens of thousands of homes every day, telling people about our total service capabilities! That personal touch had the potential to be way more effective than any marketing campaign.

"Techs who behaved respectfully toward customers were the ones getting higher ratings. They were acting as natural agents for us, making customers likely to send their family and friends to us when appliance services were needed."

What We Saw Tech Managers Doing

It would be important to coach service techs in the new customer-facing behaviors. Their tech managers were already doing ride-alongs, so Marcus decided to watch them coach techs in-home to see what they were doing.

"But what I saw them doing wouldn't help. The tech manager's goal was simply to ensure that techs worked quickly and safely: "Did the tech follow procedures to diagnose/fix the problem? Did they follow our safety protocols?"

"Unfortunately, there was zero focus on the techs' behavior with the customer! Clearly, this would be a whole new world for tech managers, to add coaching of customer-service behaviors. But it had to happen to meet our goal of making customers our advocates. This would be a major culture change."

Step 3: Clarify Vital Behaviors
What Behaviors Are Needed Most from Service Techs and Tech Managers?

Marcus and his team gathered extensive input from customers and service techs and their managers from across the organization to nail down the small number of truly Vital Behaviors needed. They then created the acronyms PREDICT and CORE to help service techs and tech managers remember what to do:

Service Technician Vital Behaviors—
These behaviors PREDICT a legendary customer experience:

P repare: At the warehouse, make sure you have all needed parts on your truck for today's customer manifest.

R apport: Establish immediate trust with customers when you greet them before entering their home.

E xplain: Confirm the customer's repair needs and explain what you'll be doing to make repairs.

D emonstrate: Engage the customer in demonstrating that their product is fixed and working properly.

I nform: Share with the customer helpful information about their product and other products that we can service.

C lean-Up: Leave the customer's home as clean as when you entered.

T emperature Check: Watch for customer dissatisfaction and address it right away. Encourage customer to complete the satisfaction questionnaire (without pressure to respond in a certain way).

Tech Manager Vital Behaviors—
These behaviors are CORE to being a great coach to service technicians:

C onduct Customer Observation Rides with each tech (complete xx per month).

O bserve Customer Responses for signs of satisfaction or dissatisfaction with the tech's behavior.

R einforce the Vital Behaviors the tech actually did, and redirect any undesired behaviors.

E xplore the Tech's Take on the Visit, compared to the customer's, to discover hints the customer gave to indicate their satisfaction level and how the tech handled it. (Do this in the truck immediately afterwards.)

Step 4: "Wire" Ally Feedback Loops
How Can We Get Customer Feedback to Techs Immediately After Every Visit?

The next question was: "How do we get the 8,000 techs to consistently perform these Vital Behaviors on every home visit?" The answer was simple: Give them timely performance feedback, directly from their customers. Marcus said,

"It was critical to give techs immediate feedback on how they did with each customer, ASAP after the visit. If techs received feedback even a few hours after a service call, they forgot the details of what happened, so the feedback lost its punch. So, essential to our success was for the techs to promptly hear 'How well I did.' The challenge became how to get feedback from the customer, and then deliver it to the tech immediately after each service call."

They put in place two primary feedback loops for the techs:

1. Customer satisfaction questionnaire.

To collect feedback, we created a short In-Home Customer Satisfaction (CSAT) Questionnaire that was based on the Vital Behaviors we wanted our customers to see the tech doing. Marcus says they always put the customer's convenience first:

"We gave customers an easy way to enter their ratings directly on the tech's tablet computer at the end of the service call. We stressed that it was important that the tech not pressure the customer to respond in a certain way."

We talked with Larry, a service technician, who agreed:

"Everyone hates when someone gives you a customer satisfaction survey and says, 'I'd appreciate it if you'd give us 5 stars, because our bonuses depend on it.'"

> **In-Home Customer Satisfaction (CSAT) Questionnaire**
>
> Please rate your service experience on a scale of 1 to 5, with 5 being the highest (best).
>
> 1. How satisfied are you with the care shown by the Technician for your home and products?
> 2. How would you rate the Technician who was in your home in terms of treating you as a valued customer?
> 3. How satisfied are you with the way the Technician explained the needed repair and cost?
> 4. How would you rate the Technician's professional appearance and attitude?
> 5. How would you rate the Technician who was in your home on making you aware of other products or services we provide?
> 6. Based on your overall experience, how likely are you to recommend us to a friend or relative?

Marcus and the technicians tested different ways to introduce the survey to customers. They started with a simple script that everyone could customize:

"Customer Satisfaction is important to us at In-Home ApplianceTech. We ask every customer to complete a very short survey at the end of every visit. Your ratings will never be used against me or anyone else. They will be used to help us know what we did well and how we can improve.

"I'm going to clean up and get my tools packed. You can leave the tablet on the counter after you are done."

When the technicians retrieved the tablet, they said something like:

"Thank you so much for helping us be the best we can be. We want to earn the right to be your number-one choice for in-home appliance repair."

Marcus adds,

"Then, the tech received feedback on their mobile device ASAP after each visit. We took extra precautions to make sure the feedback didn't pop up while the tech was driving! We also made sure the feedback identified the customer so the tech would instantly remember."

2. Feedback and coaching from tech managers.

One big factor in the success of this initiative was to repurpose and rename the ride-alongs. The original purpose of ride-alongs was for the manager to observe the tech in-home to make sure they worked quickly and safely. For this new Net Promoter Score effort, they were turned into "Customer Observation Rides," where managers observed the customer's reactions to the tech.

Managers focused mainly on helping the tech do the last Vital Behavior in the PREDICT Model: Temperature Check. The techs needed to learn to observe customers to see if they were satisfied and adjust if they were not. The tech managers taught them how to do service recovery in-the-moment to get the customer back into the Promoter zone. The managers coached techs:

"As you're explaining things to the customer, observe their facial expression. If you see any sign of dissatisfaction or confusion, stop and ask if they have a question or concern."

After an in-home customer visit, the tech manager might say,

"Hey, when you were explaining the reasons for the repair, did you notice that Mr. Smith frowned and had a quizzical look on his face? That was your cue to pause and ask if he had any questions."

Marcus notes,

"We tripled the number of customer observation rides for managers so they could watch their techs doing the new Vital Behaviors, as well as continue to coach on safety and operational processes. Throughout the program, a technician could ask for a customer observation ride. Those who requested rides showed marked improvements in their Net Promoter Scores."

Step 5: Build Habits Using 3 Pillars
How Can We Get Techs the Support They Need to Change Their Behaviors?

Marcus says that one of the biggest challenges was getting buy-in:

"Techs and their managers doubted whether this behavior-change effort was needed. Just because the division leaders had a smart solution didn't mean everyone would buy-in and cooperate!

"It was hard to get techs and managers to adopt these new Vital Behaviors, perform them consistently, and sustain them, for a classic reason: it meant changing habits and doing some unfamiliar things while also maintaining busy repair schedules."

Marcus's expertise in Behavior Science was the engine that made it happen. He purposefully wove together the 3 Pillars for enabling behavior change:

1. **Make sure behavioral expectations are always clear.**

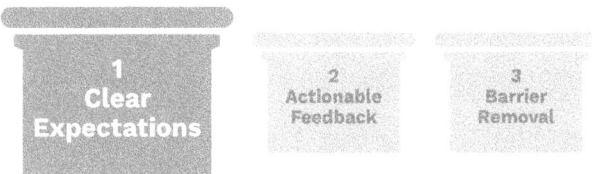

Marcus did four things to make sure expectations were very clear for the 8,000 techs and their 450 managers:

- **Consistently and widely communicate the importance of tech behavior in creating loyal customers.**

    "We knew that behavior accounted for 80% of the difference between customers who were willing to recommend us and those who weren't. That was a big 'Aha!' for everyone. We shared this research broadly and stressed the importance of behavior in every presentation about this effort, from board-level to store-level. We painted a sharp picture in everyone's mind about which elements of the customer experience were behavioral. This became a whole new way of looking at things, and it was part of the magic."

- **Train with lots of practice.**

  Hands-on training was required to jump-start the Vital Behaviors. It required active practice through role-plays based on common service scenarios. During training, techs became comfortable with being coached on these behaviors. And managers became comfortable using the **CORE** coaching model to help techs implement the **PREDICT** customer service behaviors.

- **Use small behavior goals to start.**

  Back on the job, techs started with easy behavior goals, and then advanced to harder ones. Initially, everyone did this together. For example, the second Vital Behavior in the PREDICT Model was to quickly establish rapport with the customer. Thousands of techs agreed to start the visit by asking, "Do you mind if I put on these booties, so I don't track dirt into your home?" They already used booties anyway, so the additional behavior of "telling the customer why" was easy to do. And customers really appreciated it. Techs could see the positive impact of this little behavior right away.

- **Share success stories from opinion leaders.**

  Marcus and his team set up a communication system so opinion leaders among the techs could share their success stories about which specific behaviors improved customer satisfaction scores. Having these well-respected opinion leaders talk about their outcomes was powerful. For example:

"Mrs. Smith's job ticket said her refrigerator wasn't cooling properly. As I replaced the thermostat, I asked, 'Have you noticed any other problems?' And she said, 'Oh yes, glad you asked—it wasn't making ice even before this cooling problem happened. And I'm hosting a dinner party this weekend!' I would not have known that unless I asked about issues beyond what was on the service order. She gave me a 10 on our survey."

Stories like this made the behaviors very real: "I tried this behavior. I had a positive outcome. You should try it too."

2. **Make sure feedback loops are working.**

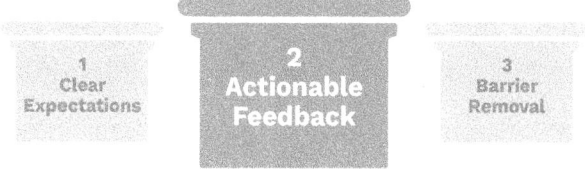

- **Make the customer feedback more effective.**

    In the initial days of the program, not all customers were willing to fill out the questionnaire on the tech's tablet computer. Marcus knew how important it was to get feedback from as many customers as possible, so he and his team made some adjustments.

    "We created multiple ways for customers to complete the Customer Satisfaction Questionnaire. We made it available by email and text messaging. If we didn't get a response, our Call Center followed up. As a result, we achieved very high response rates, so our techs knew the data were valid."

- **Change how they start shifts and management meetings.**

    Tech managers changed the way they started their shifts by asking techs to share customer stories from the prior day. They used a format: "Here's the situation, here's what I did, this was the outcome, here's how the customer felt, and here's the score I got." These stories provided the opportunity for leaders and coworkers to provide feedback to each other every day. They also served to broaden the pool of opinion leaders within work teams.

    Mid-level managers and executives made similar changes. They started their management meetings by asking for the same type of stories. Mid-level managers asked the tech managers to share stories about their latest customer observation visits. And executives asked mid-level managers to tell them customer stories they were hearing from the field. Such stories were shared across the company and made the Vital Behaviors come alive at all levels. They also provided a forum for leaders and techs to reinforce the importance of the overall effort daily.

3. **Make sure barriers are removed quickly.**

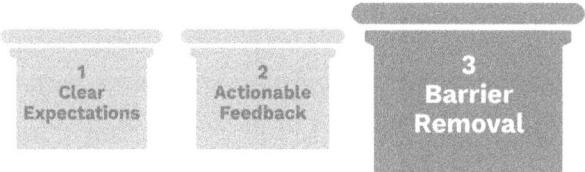

The techs and the overall project team members surfaced three big system-level barriers, and they were interrelated. Project teams were formed to address these barriers:

- **Call centers needed to capture accurate info for techs.**

  Customers dialing the Call Center typically offered minimal information: "My dryer made this funny noise, and then it stopped working," or "My stove is broken." Each of those examples could have many causes. Call Center workers did their best to record symptoms and feed them to the tech: "Here are likely things for you to investigate." But the helpfulness of the information they gathered was highly variable.

  Techs had to diagnose the problem anyway, once they were in the home. But having clear customer-reported symptoms upfront got them closer to fixing the problem sooner and told them what parts they might need to bring along. A team was formed to help call center personnel capture more meaningful details.

- **Logistics needed to get the right parts, at the right time, to the right customer's house.**

  Techs' trucks were mobile warehouses of parts for many appliances and brands. Of course, they'd never have 100% of everything needed, but as backup they also had the area warehouse, local supply stores, and other techs who were between jobs who could run and get parts. Marcus comments,

  "As you can imagine, it was a logistical nightmare. Better symptom reporting from the Call Center would help. But the techs also needed a fix for how to get parts quickly when they were in a house and had an unexpected parts need. A team was assigned to work on this process issue."

- **Techs had operational efficiency numbers to meet.**

  Techs had to get into the customer's home, troubleshoot the problem, install replacement parts, verify that the appliance was working properly, perform any cleanup from their work (old parts, packaging, spills, and anything they tracked in), present the invoice to the customer, receive payment, and ask the customer to complete the satisfaction survey.

  Any additional time spent with the customer challenged their operational efficiency numbers, so there was general resistance from executives, operational leaders, and the techs. The techs said, "We'll do this, so long as it doesn't hurt our numbers."

  Marcus notes,

"Their pushback was positive. Techs didn't say, 'No, we can't do that.' It was more like, 'Let's figure out how to make this work.' The project team did time-and-motion studies on different types of services but found that the additional focus on customer service didn't add time. Just to make sure the techs knew that we heard their concerns, we renamed the core efficiency metric from 'time-in-house' to 'time-in-house-as-needed.' In the end, it all worked out."

The Payoff: Remarkable Results

There were four big results. Marcus explains:

"First, the next year we updated our Net Promoter Score and were delighted to see a 960 basis-point lift, or *about 10%*, which was huge! When we started, our NPS was below the midpoint relative to our competitors. We not only rose above the midpoint, but became leading-edge—we became one of the higher performers among our competition. In one year!

"Second, a huge benefit of boosting our NPS was that we started reselling our in-home appliance repair services to big-box retailers and home appliance insurance companies. Those companies didn't want to talk with us without that NPS improvement.

"Third, we calculated the ROI (Return on Investment) for the program, as well as the additional sales, and both numbers confirmed that we had made a wise choice to focus on a behavior solution.

"And fourth, results were so good that eventually all the customer-facing teams at In-Home ApplianceTech joined our behavior-focused improvement program. The install teams, delivery teams, repair teams, and Call Centers—all were underneath In-Home, so we identified Vital Behaviors for all of them.

"We even extended the program to our third-party vendors. We taught their leadership how to use our approach for free in exchange for doing it with our customers first!

"I'm proud to say that many elements of the program are still up and running 15 years later."

Figure 19 shows the Vital Behavior Blueprint for Service Technicians.

*For Vital Behaviors by Service Technicians, please see the PREDICT graphic on page 137.

Figure 19

12

Nursing Home Rehabilitates Its Reputation from "Stay Away!" to "The Place to Stay!"

Caring Harmony

Medication errors:	↓70%
Agency nurse costs:	↓45%
Call-offs:	↓25%
EE engagement:	↑21pts
Private-pay beds:	↑15%

Nursing Homes Are Insanely Challenging

Nursing homes are among the most challenged of healthcare institutions. They serve our most vulnerable and beloved population: Our senior-citizen parents, grandparents, and friends. These people have paid their dues, raised generations, worked alongside us, and some even served in wartime. As they approach the sunset, they require everything from assisted living, through skilled nursing, to hospice care. And their care pulls at the heartstrings of us all, including nursing home staff.

Skilled nursing facilities today are under relentless pressure from all sides: A growing population of aging clients, a vocal group of family members deeply invested in their loved one's care, hard-to-retain staff, and above all: Maintaining senior care excellence while running the difficult business side in a fiscally sound way.

And that is the focus of this true story about a well-intentioned but struggling nursing facility named Caring Harmony that righted the ship by using Vital Behaviors.

Caring Harmony's Mission

Caring Harmony is a faith-based nursing home with a noble mission:

"We provide person-centered, compassionate care in a restful setting that promotes independence, enhances residents emotionally and spiritually, and respects their preferences."

The leadership team, along with 150 dedicated employees and numerous volunteers, were wholeheartedly devoted to ensuring that every resident experienced the highest quality of life during their final years. Many of these residents were familiar faces, such as retired church employees and community members. The staff made it a priority to uphold the values of dignity and respect for all, irrespective of financial means or prior roles before joining the home.

At the time of this story, Caring Harmony was led by a dedicated Board of Directors. Many were church members themselves. Most knew healthcare; they included the CEO of a regional hospital and the head of a large multistate health insurer. The board had worked closely with the facility's leadership on healthcare-education projects, and they were committed to helping Caring Harmony deliver the area's best care.

Sustaining Caring Harmony

Although its faith-based mission was top priority, Caring Harmony had to be financially self-sustaining for the long term. Some church members volunteered because of their commitment to the mission, but those on the staff and other healthcare professionals had to be paid. The goal was to become self-sustaining by managing the patient mix to include charity care, government-funded residents, and private-pay residents (privately insured or self-funded).

Unfortunately, a few years after Caring Harmony's founding, they were running in the red, with no improvement in sight. And there were significant operational and management problems. Employee turnover exceeded national standards. Absenteeism was high, which inevitably led to errors in care.

Every nursing home across the country experienced the same challenges. In some cases, leaders in long-term care just accepted it as part of doing business. But not the leadership of Caring Harmony—they knew things had to change.

Recognizing the need for a more professional management team, they formed a management partnership with PeakCare Network. PeakCare had deep experience in managing assisted living communities, nursing homes, and rehabilitation centers. They pledged to collaborate with Caring Harmony's Board and leadership to maintain its unique identity and mission while turning it into a financially viable, sustainable entity.

Soon, a veteran administrator from PeakCare became Caring Harmony's CEO. "Maria" had strong experience in healthcare management, and everyone hoped she would help the organization make things right.

A Maelstrom of Challenges

When Maria arrived, she immediately was confronted with issues:

"I was an outsider, inserted to lead a faith-based organization. I was from a different faith, so an immediate question was: Could I lead Caring Harmony in a way that supported their spiritual mission while simultaneously managing the business to build financial sustainability?

"The board and church volunteers felt compelled to stay deeply involved—to make sure I focused on their mission and vision. However, we lacked clear boundaries for who-does-what. They would walk the halls daily and do things the management team should be doing, like directing work and making process changes.

"I understood that their actions came from the heart, but it made my job difficult! Their continuing involvement in operations and management found us tripping over each other. Everyone meant well, but had strong opinions about what to do. So, I bobbed along in this ocean of currents, doing my best to steer the organization.

"But the overriding reality was that nursing home administration is highly regulated and complex, including rigorous periodic inspections. We *had* to change to survive."

And Then Things Went Critical

Soon the organization was shaken by serious adverse events. In moments of distraction, a few staff members didn't follow procedures and the safety of patients was put at risk. Clearly, it was time for immediate change.

One board member proposed some quick action. He had used a consulting firm to great success in improving his company's performance. The firm was CLG (cofounded by Julie Smith, this book's coauthor). They were Behavior Science experts who specialized in aligning daily actions across an organization to get strategic results. So, the board asked Julie to make a presentation to share how they created organizational behavior change. Maria recalls,

"The consultants said they would help us clarify roles and get everyone aligned to our goals. Then we would zero in on mission-critical behaviors, determining who needed to do what. They called this 'pinpointing' the behaviors. (An example behavior: *Answer a resident's call bell within 30 seconds.*)

"Everyone, including me, would have a Coaching Action Plan to help us consistently do those behaviors. As leaders, we would be responsible for creating the right environment to make sure the behaviors flourished and to sustain the improvements we would see."

The board decided to contract with the consultants. But Maria said she wasn't completely onboard at first:

"Honestly, I was a little skeptical. We had so many financial challenges that I didn't think we needed another expense, especially for this consulting help.

"I remember my first one-on-one meeting with Julie. I asked her, 'Am I the right person to help lead us through this cultural challenge? I'm not sure the organization will accept an outsider at the helm.'

"But Julie assured me that everyone would learn that Caring Harmony could both meet the mission and sustain the bottom line—it wasn't an either/or thing. People would come to see these two goals were not incompatible.

"She also said we could recoup our consulting investment within the first four months if we carefully chose financial targets, like reducing use of agency nurses. These temps cost 250% more than full-time nurses!

"So, I decided to have faith in the process. What did we have to lose?"

Building a Vital Behavior Blueprint for Success

And so the project began. The lead consultants were Julie and her colleague, Carolina. They worked hand-in-glove with Maria and Caring Harmony's Board, leaders, and employees to help people turn their good intentions into aligned actions.

In the following pages, you can see the critical path that was followed: The 5 Steps to build the Vital Behavior Blueprint so badly needed by Caring Harmony.

 ### Step 1: Prioritize Behavior-Powered Results *Which Results Will Most Improve Caring Harmony's Sustainability?*

In a major turnaround like this, Julie and Carolina knew that the client can easily bite off more than they can chew. So, they worked with Maria and Caring Harmony's leadership to prioritize all they were trying to achieve, then helped them pick the top three goals that could be improved through the aligned actions of Caring Harmony's people. Carolina notes,

"It was essential to engage as many people as possible in prioritizing, so we sent a survey to everyone: 'Tell us what issues you see, and which ones can be addressed by each of us doing things in a different way?'

"Then we did one-on-one interviews at all levels and held focus groups with front-line employees and their leaders. We also reviewed hard data from resident and family surveys, financial info, and exit interviews from departing employees."

Eventually, it all boiled down to Caring Harmony balancing "The Big Three Goals" shown below (including how to measure whether the organization was succeeding):

Become the residential care provider of choice in the area (measurable proof: Improved safety and quality outcomes and family/resident satisfaction survey results)

Become the employer of choice in the area (measurable proof: Increased staff retention and improved results on employee surveys)

Become financially viable (measurable proof: Decreased use of temporary agency nurses, and increased private-pay beds and reimbursement for higher-level services)

Maria talks about how the goals were interrelated:

"To achieve Goal #1 (Become the Residential Care Provider of Choice), everyone had to comply with our safety and quality protocols. That would be easier if we had less staff turnover, which meant achieving Goal #2 (Become the Employer of Choice).

"We needed full-time nurses who stayed and were committed to living our mission to deliver high-quality services in a faith-based environment. So, we had to reduce our reliance on temporary agency nurses, because they could never create the culture we wanted, being at Caring Harmony only briefly.

"Toward Goal #3 (Become Financially Viable), 60% of our nursing costs came from temporary agencies. If we could reduce that to 15%, we would pay for CLG's services within four months, a big jump toward achieving Goal #3.

"Financial viability also meant making sure we were fully reimbursed for services. That required record-keeping that was current and accurate so we could promptly bill insurance or clients for reimbursement. If a patient suddenly needed complex wound management that required more expensive skilled nursing care, we had to make sure we coded that service accurately in the medical records for reimbursement."

Carolina says that discussing these goals wasn't easy:

"Clearly, we had to keep the lights on, yet some of Caring Harmony's leadership felt passionately that we shouldn't be so focused on the business side. Maria was so calm during these discussions—I don't know how she did it."

Maria began to see how the process could work:

"Ultimately, everyone saw that we had to balance all three goals because they were so intertwined. And people began to see that we could balance our goals only if we were all aligned. So, we spent a lot of time cascading The Big Three Goals down to each department, so everyone knew how their group contributed. That led to the next phase of work: Who needed to do what differently to achieve results."

Step 2: Identify Key Performer Groups
Whose Behaviors Will Most Enhance Meeting Our Goals?

"Julie and Carolina helped us clarify roles and set boundaries," Maria says. "We designated five 'Key Performer Groups,' and then defined roles and responsibilities within each group." Here are the five groups of Key Performers:

The board. Set strategy and organizational goals, respond to crises within the organization, lead any acquisitions and mergers, support executive duties, and hire/fire/evaluate senior leaders and establish their compensation.

Caring Harmony leaders. Establish core systems and processes that meet all regulations and manage them daily to achieve the Big Three Goals.

Department teams. Meet departmental goals, and help other departments meet theirs too. There were three departmental groups: Administration (executive team, admin staff, billing coders), Direct Care Staff (nursing, nurse billing coders, physical therapy, social work, activities), and Support Staff (food services, housekeeping, maintenance, groundskeeping).

Volunteers. Support Caring Harmony's mission and vision through volunteer work.

Everyone. Consistently demonstrate to residents, families, and employees that Caring Harmony was the best possible place to live and work.

Step 3: Clarify Vital Behaviors
What Behaviors Were Needed Most from Each Key Performer Group?

During the interviews and focus groups, Carolina collected examples of behaviors required to meet the organization's goals. Three buckets of behaviors emerged: Cross-Cutting Behaviors—things everyone in the organization needed to do; Departmental Behaviors—things each department had to do; and Leader Behaviors—things leaders needed to do to reinforce desired behaviors of employees. Here is a look at each bucket:

1. **Cross-cutting behaviors.** There were three pinpointed behaviors everyone needed to do, from the board to the frontline.

    - **Answer Resident's Call Bells Within 30 Seconds.** No matter who you were, if you heard a resident's call bell sound, you owned it. If they needed a glass of water or their TV remote, you got it. If they needed greater help, you summoned someone to assist. This behavior alone made a huge difference in Caring Harmony's family and resident satisfaction scores, because people felt they were being heard by a very responsive staff.

- **Use the Chain of Command to Problem-Solve Issues.** The chain of command was badly broken. Rather than taking issues up the chain, people talked behind each other's backs or escalated things directly to the board or the church leaders. So it became a Vital Behavior at all levels to take issues to the right place for resolution.

- **Problem-Solve Issues Objectively.** When someone raises an issue, don't jump to conclusions. Instead, help them make their thinking visible and objectively define the problem, make your own thinking visible about what you heard them say, and your view of what could be happening, and summarize key points to advance the discussion toward the best solution.

2. **Departmental behaviors.** Carolina and Maria worked with each department to pinpoint the most critical behaviors everyone needed to do to achieve the Big Three Goals. Carolina says these pinpointed behaviors focused mainly on implementing existing standards of care:

"We focused on everything needed to achieve Goal #1 (Become the Residential Care Provider of Choice). Fortunately, most things that direct care teams needed to do were already laid out. But the problem was behavioral—the teams didn't follow the processes and procedures consistently or promptly.

"For example, direct care teams needed to meet with families monthly to review the care plan for their loved ones, but that didn't always happen. Or they needed to follow stringent medication delivery to ensure that the *right* medication, and *right* dose, was delivered to the *right* person, at the *right* time, using the *right* routing system every time and documented. But these things weren't consistently happening."

Maria describes the realities faced by care teams:

"The protocols were clear enough, but when you have 120 patients on multiple medications, assuring accurate medication delivery is a big challenge. It is in every healthcare environment. You must focus. And that's what we helped everyone do: Focus on doing things the right way, every time."

Carolina remembers the multitude of focus areas for direct care teams:

"It was a lot of things. Safety checks, body audits for bed sores, deep cleaning of rooms, conducting patient rounds for high-risk patients, and being diligent about shift handoffs so the next shift knew about any changes in the residents' conditions. All that."

Maria recalls working with Human Resources (HR) on Goal #2 (Become the Employer of Choice):

"They identified essential HR behaviors needed to quickly select and onboard new employees. Things like confirming within 24 hours that they had received an applicant's resume, or letting the applicant know within 48 hours of the interview whether they had been selected.

"HR also needed to communicate better with the direct care teams. People in the units wanted to know when their coworkers were hired, terminated, or voluntarily left. From their perspective, if they showed up for a shift and someone was not there, what had happened? We stopped a lot of rumors and increased employee engagement by being transparent."

Maria worked personally with direct care teams and administration to achieve Goal #3 (Become Financially Viable):

"Care teams needed to assess and update residents' care needs promptly, and administration personnel needed to get care changes approved quickly so they could be implemented—not only to benefit patients, but for us to capture reimbursements.

"Coding is extremely complex. We found that we had to get very detailed about daily coding to ensure codes were updated correctly by both direct care teams and administration. If we missed a day, it was not serving the patients, plus we could never recoup that reimbursement.

"We started something new with the certified nurse assistants. Because they had the most contact with residents, we met with them monthly to see whether they had discovered problems other care team members missed. Often, they had. This monthly check-in highlighted the importance of looking for changes in their patients every day and reporting those changes quickly. It made them a key part of the care team."

3. **Leader behaviors.** For the third bucket, leaders had to provide regular feedback to reinforce how important the cross-cutting and departmental behaviors were. This was the only way these behaviors could become habit or hardwired. Maria says,

"To achieve this, we had leaders do 'walkabouts' daily and talk with people to see what was going on at the behavioral level. We also set a goal for leaders to talk with each employee at least monthly to learn how their personal Coaching Action Plan was going."

Not only did Maria set the expectation that leaders needed to be very visible in the halls every day, but she role-modeled it, despite a heavy administrative load. Seeing her level of commitment was inspiring to everyone.

"It was hard initially to fit that into my schedule. But the time I used to spend on fire-fighting soon got shifted into time for walkabouts, where I could reinforce the actions that prevented problems. Very soon, the leader-employee feedback loops became a strong and fundamental part of our leadership systems because everyone experienced the benefits."

Here are examples of Vital Behaviors for this project:

Leader Vital Behaviors
- Conduct daily walkabouts to observe behavior, give employees feedback, and identify issues.
- Meet with every employee at least monthly to review their Coaching Action Plans.
- Review progress on problem-solving, behaviors, and results at every regularly scheduled management meeting.

Departmental Vital Behaviors

Sample:
- Assess patient's condition daily to update billing codes so proper care can be provided.
- Follow safe lifting procedures.
- If you see something wrong, say something.
- If you call off, do so at least 16 hours before your scheduled shift.

Cross-Cutting Vital Behaviors
- Answer resident's call bells within 30 seconds.
- Use the chain of command to problem-solve issues.
- Problem-solve issues objectively.

Step 4: "Wire" Ally Feedback Loops
What Feedback Loops Were Most Critical to Success?

Maria notes,

"We really promoted the value of feedback. One of our mantras was feedback is a gift. Carolina taught us that. We said that constructive feedback is the biggest gift of all because it helps people grow. That way of thinking began to permeate the organization."

They put in place four primary feedback loops between Allies:

1. **Feedback from each leader to their direct reports.** Leaders were expected to be out daily in the work units, giving employees feedback. They were also to meet with their employees monthly to update their individual Coaching Action Plans. These feedback loops grew very strong and produced tremendous trust between leaders and employees.

2. **Feedback from leader to leader.**
   - **Individual leader coaching and feedback.** For the first six months, Carolina coached the leaders. Then she trained internal people as Leader Coaches, who helped leaders coach their employees and each other.
   - **Leadership assessments.** Every leader got quarterly 360° feedback from their own leader, direct reports, and peers. This feedback focused on how well they were doing in giving their people the right performance support. Leader Coaches helped leaders use this feedback to develop their own Coaching Action Plans to become better leaders.

- **Management meetings.** Maria met with the management team weekly to review progress and problem-solve. Everyone was expected to share what they learned during their walkabouts: What behaviors were going well? What behaviors did you reinforce or redirect? What Coaching Action Plans were updated? What problems were resolved or still pending?

3. **Feedback from residents/families to everyone.** The surveys coming from residents and families were reviewed monthly in every department, in the management meeting, and at the board level so leaders could directly see the impact on Caring Harmony's clients.

4. **Feedback from employees to the organization.** Annual employee engagement surveys were reviewed at every level and action plans for continuous improvement were put in place.

Carolina emphasized the power of Maria's leadership:

"She was an amazing champion. She had one-on-one meetings with managers, asking to see their Coaching Action Plans. She demonstrated the discipline to carve out substantial time to say, 'Let's talk about what you've done to help your team with call-offs or with medication delivery.' She was diligent about using the Coaching Action Plans to guide discussions."

Maria explained how challenging those discussions were:

"Our people are so committed to our organization, and are really well-meaning. But to professionalize their roles, set and review goals, reinforce behaviors, comply with government and legal requirements, and hold people accountable—that part was very difficult. I'm really proud of how we made those discussions routine, positive, and helpful."

Step 5: Build Habits Using 3 Pillars
How Can We Get Everyone the Support They Need to Sustain New Vital Behaviors?

As the program unfolded, powerful alignment grew up and down the organization. Remarkably, all of the Big Three Goals dramatically improved within six months, so Maria shifted from fire-fighting to keeping the momentum going.

"It's one thing to have a program like this succeed when all eyes are on it, and we had a consulting group here to help. But now we needed to sustain it on our own, to keep it working. We had to continue the focus on behavior, results, feedback, and positive accountability."

So, going forward, leaders were expected to provide their employees with the 3 Pillars:

1. **Make sure behavioral expectations are always clear.**

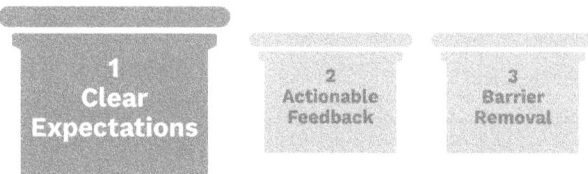

- **Make it clear during training that we are committed to behavior-based management.** Employee onboarding was changed to immerse new hires in behavior-change concepts and tools. After onboarding, new employees understood that Caring Harmony's management practices included managing at the behavioral level. Periodic refresher sessions were held for leaders and the board to reaffirm the organization's commitment to behavior-based management and to advance their skills.

- **Keep coaching actions plans updated.** Everyone continued to have Coaching Actions Plans to help them grow and develop.

2. **Keep feedback loops working properly.**

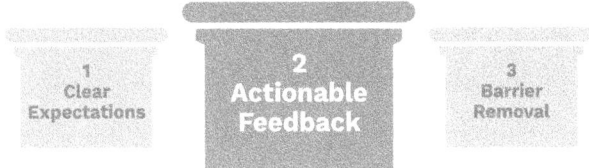

- **Use the feedback loops we built.** Caring Harmony continued to use all the feedback loops: Daily walkabouts by leaders in the units, leadership assessments, management meeting reviews of the system, individual Coaching Action Plan discussions between leaders and employees, resident/family surveys, and employee engagement surveys.

- **Fix a feedback loop if it's broken.** Since the organization was so flat, leaders could quickly see if a feedback loop was broken, and fix it. Example: If a leader was poor at giving constructive feedback, a leader coach was asked to guide them.

3. **Make sure barriers are removed quickly.**

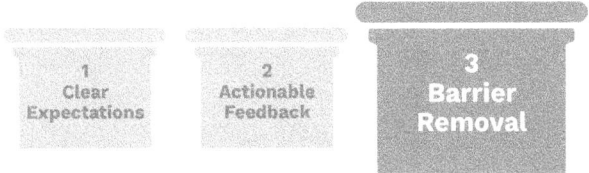

- **Continuously improve teamwork.** It's always difficult to bring together a new team and align everyone. Caring Harmony addressed this with team-building for the board and senior leaders. These leaders did memorable exercises demonstrating that they could improve things if they listened to each other and respected each other's diverse backgrounds. These sessions helped key leaders bond and surface interpersonal barriers they needed to work on.

- **Continuously improve the problem-solving process.** After the team-building sessions, they continued to work on their relationships so they could problem-solve effectively. Over time, the problem-solving process worked well, and people trusted the chain-of-command to get issues resolved.

Leaders at Caring Harmony found that this way of managing helped them adapt to changes over 15+ years. They would always ask, "Which behaviors need to flourish to make new things happen?" Then they'd update the Coaching Action Plans to make sure these new behaviors were supported. Instead of blaming people when problems arose, they focused objectively on the behaviors needed to succeed. "It just became our common world view of how to help each other get things done."

The Payoff: Remarkable Results

Results improved sharply. Within six months they achieved:

- 90%+ adherence to safety and quality procedures
- 70% fewer medication errors
- 45% decrease in agency costs
- 15% more private-pay beds
- 25% fewer call-offs
- 21-point increase in employee engagement

But most importantly, patient and family satisfaction improved, and these folks began recommending the facility to others. Maria notes:

"We are proud to say that the results were sustained over 15 years, and we won multiple awards for being the Resident Care Provider of Choice and the Employer of Choice in the area.

"When the project began, we were in turmoil. But we quickly became the 'Little Engine that Could!' For a small organization, we became pretty sophisticated, doing whatever we put our minds to."

They had done things that would have stretched the capabilities of the average nursing home. Maria shared some remarkable facts about what Caring Harmony accomplished:

- Added subspecialty services and became well-known for having a strong rehabilitation and outpatient program, even building an addition to handle increased patient volume.

- Affiliated with an area nursing school to stabilize the nursing base.

- Built a café to become a community hub for health activities and programming.

- Built a strong reputation in the surrounding communities. This resulted in robust referral relationships with marquee healthcare systems.

Maria summed it up with pride:

"Whenever we had management turnover, we saw it as an opportunity—a chance to select replacements who had a background in managing long-term care facilities. Because our newly hired managers loved our culture, they stayed long-term, so we enjoyed a seasoned, professional management team.

"Many of us have since retired, but we still meet several times a year to reminisce. At our last get-together, one retiree noted, 'Those years together were Camelot.'

"It was a once-in-a-lifetime opportunity for a wonderful team to flourish and make a difference in people's lives. We truly learned how to balance our mission with the management of Caring Harmony. And everyone felt so proud to be part of that."

Figure 20 shows the Vital Behavior Blueprint for everyone.

CASE STUDY: CARING HARMONY
Vital Behavior Blueprint

* *For Vital Behaviors by these Key Performers, please see graphics on page 161.*

Figure 20

BEYOND BASICS

Demystifying the Science and Art Behind Our Success

We've both had the privilege of helping numerous companies deploy behavior-based performance improvement strategies, resulting in remarkable outcomes that left our clients thrilled. However, not every client has cared about the solid science behind our methods. Instead, they would use our methods selectively, whenever they needed to achieve success on specific projects.

Yet, some clients were curious, wanting a deeper understanding of the underlying principles behind our work after witnessing its effectiveness. They sought to apply it more broadly and independently. In response, we helped these organizations learn about the science behind behavior-based improvement. Over time, these companies ingrained behavior-based practices into their culture, making it an integral component of their operations and driving exceptional performance year after year.

This section provides insights on elevating your organization from achieving success on targeted projects to consistently delivering exceptional performance across all endeavors.

13

Behavior Analysis: The Science of *Individual* Behavior Change

Behavior Analysis Underpins Our Approach

Psychology has many different sub-disciplines, all focused on better understanding human behavior. These sub-disciplines include social psychology, psychobiology, neuroscience, behavioral economics, cognitive psychology, and Behavior Analysis—lots of interesting stuff.

In this ocean of knowledge, we chose Behavior Analysis for our core models and methods. Why? Quite simply, because *Behavior Analysis is the science of what works in behavior change.*

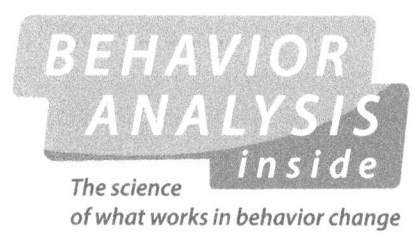

The science of what works in behavior change

Behavior Analysis has proven effective across diverse domains, including healthcare, education, sports, business, addictions, and criminal justice, delivering successful outcomes for individuals and organizations. Its principles underpin disciplines like behavioral economics, behavioral medicine, and behavior-based safety. Decades of successful applications like these have established Behavior Analysis as one of the most robust and scientifically respected approaches to behavior improvement today.

We mentioned in our introduction (Our Discovery of the Science and Art of Vital Behaviors) that we both fell in love with Behavior Analysis because it takes a non-blaming perspective on understanding human behavior. Rather than blaming the individual for bad behavior, it focuses on understanding an individual's observable behaviors and how the external environment promotes or hinders desired behaviors.

Behavior Analysis provides the way for organizations to "drive out fear," which is one of the "14 Points for Management" developed by business management guru Dr. W. Edward Deming. He said that modern behavioral psychology had demonstrated that fear destroys motivation, and remnants of fear cause resentment and resistance. Many people have called this his "elusive" principle because he did not provide a way to drive out fear, like he did for his other Points. Behavior Analysis provides the systematic way to do this. It's a positive approach that helps people focus on what they want, rather than the fear they wish to avoid.

A Basic Habit Formation Model for Individuals

If you are seeking a simple way to get started, these best-selling books (such as *Atomic Habits* by James Clear, *The Power of Habit* by Charles Duhigg, and *Tiny Habits* by B.J. Fogg) provide practical ways for individuals to break old habits and make new ones. These authors have done a wonderful job of converting Behavior Analysis research into simple tools that anyone can use to succeed at behavior change.

These popular books all present a similar basic Habit Formation Model to guide individuals through behavior change (Figure 21). In a nutshell, habits (good or bad) are formed mainly by the external environment that surrounds you. Environmental cues happen before a behavior (or new, desired habit) and prompt you to start doing the behavior. Rewards come after the behavior and provide you with a positive payoff, so you want to do the behavior again.

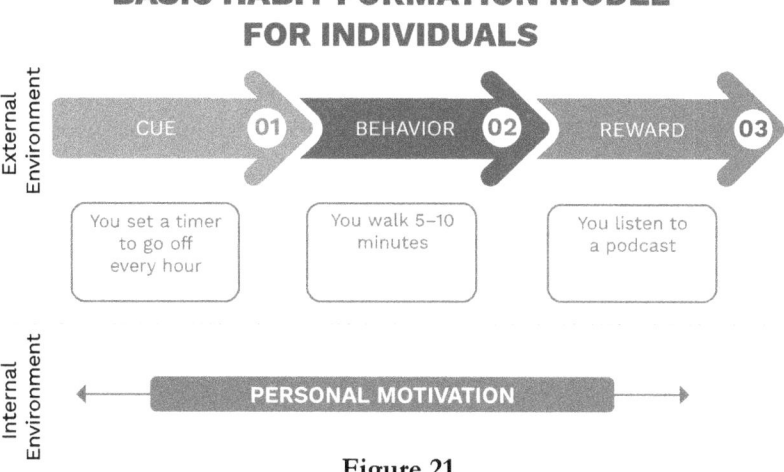

Figure 21

Of course, we all have private thoughts and feelings, known only to us. This personal motivation is an important part of habit change too. It includes your desire and ability to do the new behavior, and your belief that it will be worth it (will the rewards be there?). It also includes how you feel before and after the behavior.

Here's how it works: Let's say you've heard people say, "Sitting is the new smoking," meaning the behavior of sitting too much can ruin your health. That worries you because you sit all day at your job. How can you make yourself a new habit to get up periodically and walk around? You create that new habit, like this:

- **Cue.** Set your phone's timer to go off every two hours. That is your nudge to do your new habit.

- **Behavior.** When the alarm goes off, your new habit is to stand up and walk around for 10 minutes. (You decide to start small by walking for only 5 minutes.)

- **Reward.** You listen to podcasts while you walk around, which is a treat for you! Over time, you form a new habit that you look forward to doing.

But What About Your Personal Motivation?

All three book authors (Clear, Duhigg, and Fogg) stress that the external environment is more important than internal, personal motivation—because if you change your environment, behavior change will follow, and so will a change in your thoughts and beliefs.

In the example above (standing up and walking every hour), your internal starting thought might be, "I'll give it a try, but I never stick with anything." However, as you try the new routine, if you've found the right rewards, your thoughts will change to, "I can do this! I'm learning new things on my walks, and I love the breaks." Your personal motivation level will change as you succeed in making small changes. By directly changing the external factors, you often influence the internal factors, like your thoughts and beliefs.

The Advanced Habit Formation Model for Individuals

We owe a debt of gratitude to the authors of these books. They are helping people realize that environmental cues and rewards strongly influence whether they have good habits or bad ones—and most importantly, providing simple models that anyone can understand to modify their environment for success.

Of course, for new habits to stick over the long term, the total environment needs to support the new behaviors, not just immediate cues and rewards. The example above works when things are straightforward, such as when you are working at home and have the freedom to get up and walk around every hour when your timer goes off. But what happens when you are suddenly asked to travel for your job? Or when you can't listen to your podcasts because you're on Zoom meetings more frequently than ever before? Or perhaps your boss thinks it's disruptive when you move around during Zoom meetings, even though you are still actively participating in the meeting.

No wonder 80% of New Year's resolutions are forgotten by February! Life gets in the way and the routines you thought would be simple suddenly become too hard. That's when you will have to make adjustments.

You'll have to start thinking about different ways you can still embed movement into your day. You might pack comfortable shoes for your travel days rather than just dress shoes. Or you might reconsider how to define "movement." Maybe it's 30 minutes at the beginning of your day. You also might consider other rewards you can build in, such as getting other coworkers to walk with you. It's times like these where a more advanced model can help you create new habits.

There is one core tool from Behavior Analysis that brings greater clarity to cues and rewards: The ABC Model. It is the core of Figure 22, shown in the three arrows.

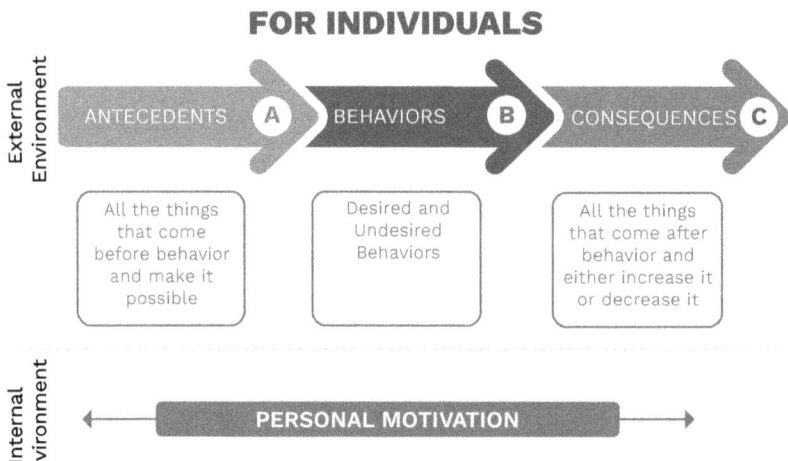

Figure 22

You can see that the terms "cues" and "rewards" are replaced with "Antecedents" and "Consequences." This is Behavior Analysis technical jargon, and it represents many more external environmental factors beyond simple cues and rewards.

- **Antecedents (A's).** These are all the things that occur before behaviors and make it possible for them to happen. Behavior Analysts look at multiple Antecedents such as the setting itself, training, equipment, what you've learned from others about what worked (or didn't), who is in the environment, what triggers or cues exist, etc.

- **Behaviors (B's).** These are the specific pinpointed behaviors that can be operationally defined and measured. You can analyze the A's and C's for both desired and undesired behaviors to see how to change bad habits and develop new, good ones.

- **Consequences (C's).** These are things that happen after the behaviors. They are the critical drivers of all behavior because they either encourage or discourage a behavior from happening again. (For example, if you get an underdesk treadmill and your boss supports you in using it during meetings, you're more likely to keep moving during the day.)

That's the *external* environment. But over the last three decades, Behavior Analysis has evolved new models to help understand how our *internal* world of emotions, thoughts, and beliefs are shaped by the external environment and affect our behaviors. These models help you understand how your thoughts and feelings are learned from others and evolve through your lived experiences. Most importantly, they help you see that you don't have to act on negative thoughts and feelings, but rather be mindful of what situations trigger them, then use strategies to remain calm. The goal is to ride alongside them, or reframe them so they don't rule you.

After 100+ years of development and testing, Behavior Analysis offers a more advanced way to nudge and support behavior change so it's sustainable. It comes with a comprehensive, well-tested scientific framework that anyone can access. This framework includes core principles, terms, tools, Laws of Behavior, and scientific methods.

If you want to become deeply knowledgeable in Behavior Analysis, there are several undergraduate and even doctoral programs you can access, as well as online certificate programs. (Want to learn more about Organizational Behavior Management (OBM)? See the section "MORE . . ." in the back of the book.)

Chapter 13 Summary

- We selected Behavior Analysis as the foundation for our 5-Step model because it's grounded in the science of effective behavior change.

- Instead of blaming individuals for their poor habits, Behavior Analysis focuses on understanding observable behaviors and how the environment can be adjusted to support desired changes.

- Simple Habit Formation Models offer strategies for individuals to establish new habits by leveraging external environmental cues and rewards.

- Internal, personal motivation is key, but if you change your environment, behavior change will follow, and so will a change in your thoughts and beliefs.

- The ABC Model is an advanced Habit Formation Model, prompting individuals to consider all factors preceding behavior (Antecedents) and those following it to either reinforce or deter its repetition (Consequences).

- Behavior Analysis offers a comprehensive scientific framework that is accessible to anyone interested in delving deeper.

14

Organizational Behavior Management (OBM): Behavior Analysis Applied in Organizations

When it comes to changing behavior on a large scale in organizations, the environmental Antecedents and Consequences are much more complex. They can come from multiple, diverse sources—like coworkers, leaders, customers, organizational systems, government, community, family, media—and there are numerous types of cues and rewards available. To deal with this complexity, 50+ years ago Behavior Analysts pioneered a whole new area called Organizational Behavior Management (OBM):

> **ORGANIZATIONAL BEHAVIOR MANAGEMENT**
> OBM is the study and application of Behavior Analysis in organizations that focuses on assessing and changing work environments to improve employee performance and business results, as well as employee engagement.

Since OBM uses Behavior Analysis as its experimental base, OBM is very different from other approaches to workplace performance improvement, such as Industrial-Organizational Psychology. Here's the difference:

- Industrial-Organizational Psychology is based on multiple theories about human behavior and focuses on topics such as personnel selection and placement.

- OBM is guided by a single theory of human behavior. Historically OBM has emphasized identifying/modifying environmental variables to improve observable employee behaviors that optimize personal and organizational results. The goal is to design system-wide Antecedents and Consequences that will produce the largest positive impact on the organization.

OBM methods have underpinned behavior-based performance improvement, training and development, behavior-based safety, pay for performance, employee health and well-being, performance coaching, behavioral interviewing, performance management, and consumer choice/behavioral economics. In all these diverse applications, OBM principles and methods have produced amazing results, as documented in numerous books and refereed journals over the past 50+ years.

We Enhanced the ABC Model to Achieve Scale

Even though OBM is powerful, in the 1990s it was still a struggle to implement it *at scale* to help organizations achieve results across sites, divisions, or even globally. To do that, we had to combine methods and tools from several disciplines beyond OBM: Change management, organizational development, management systems, operational excellence, industrial engineering, and process improvement.

This resulted in the development of an enhanced ABC Analysis, which shows the different cues and rewards that can help embed habits in organizations, from small teams to the entire company. We call this

The Extended ABC Model for Habit Formation in Organizations, and it is used for designing habits at scale. See Figure 23 for an overview of this model.

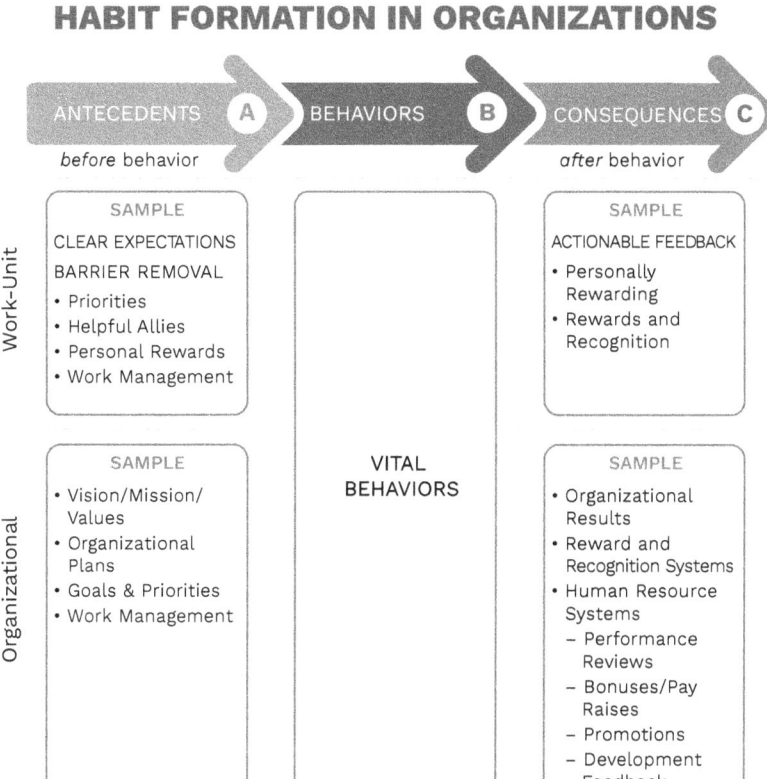

Figure 23

You can see that A's and C's can be put in place at two different levels:

The Work-Unit Level. These A's and C's tend to be available in the Key Performer's immediate work environment. Because they happen so close to the Vital Behaviors, they are more powerful than those offered by the organization. Examples include the supervisor's communication of performance expectations (goals, Vital Behaviors, work output requirements); individual, actionable performance feedback; whether other co-workers are positively supporting their Allies; etc.

The Organizational Level. These A's and C's tend to be further away or more removed from the Key Performer. They also are delivered less frequently and are more delayed. As a result, they tend to be less important to Key Performers on a daily basis. Examples include an organization's mission, vision, and values, organizational plans (strategic and business plans), training, annual performance incentives, etc.

To sustain behaviors over the long run, you need to align the A's and C's across both organizational and work-unit levels. You don't want them working against each other! For example, if your organization has prioritized safety (an Antecendent), but work unit leaders reward productivity at all costs (a Consequence), performers will be confused—and you'll be at risk of high behavior variability.

Make Sure Key Performers Have All the A's and C's They Need to Do the Vital Behaviors

There are many A's and C's available in organizations. As we know from the 3 Pillars, the most essential Antecedents are "Clear Expectations" and "Barrier Removal," and the most critical Consequence is "Actionable Feedback." This is why we listed them first in Figure 23. We know from experience that these are necessary—and are the most frequently missing elements in execution support. We recommend you start there.

Other A's and C's may be needed as well. If they are missing, they can become barriers to doing Vital Behaviors. Your job as a leader is to knock down these barriers so people can shine. We have two tools, available in our free *Vital Behavior Blueprint Templates*, that will help you determine which barriers need to be addressed:

The 3 Pillars Pulse Checks for Key Performers and Leaders. This contains questions you can ask Key Performers and their leaders to see if they are getting the enabling A's and C's they need to execute and sustain Vital Behaviors—or if barriers stand in their way that need to be removed. This pulse check is designed to be used in conversations with others, or it can be sent out as an online pulse check.

The 3 Pillars Drill-Down Pulse Check. In Figure 23 we provided a sample of A's and C's for you to consider. In the *Vital Behavior Blueprint Templates*, we provide a detailed pulse check for you to use to assess whether you have all the A's and C's needed to support new behaviors.

3 Important Facts about the ABC Model

We've asked our clients what they remember most about the ABC Model. What were their big Aha! moments?? They told us that the following three things stuck in their minds and made them more effective as leaders:

1. **Consequences are 4x more powerful than Antecedents in sustaining Vital Behaviors.** This is true for both organizational and individual behavior change. Antecedents get Vital Behaviors started, but people will only keep doing those behaviors if they pay off in some way. This makes logical sense. If no one notices or cares whether you've done a behavior, why should you continue to do it—unless it's naturally reinforcing to you? Remember this: The reward (Consequence) is 4x more powerful than the cue (Antecedent) if you want to sustain behavior change.

2. **If your organization struggles with adherence or accountability, it's almost always a Consequence issue.** Despite this, most organizations do very little to manage Consequences. Instead, they focus 80% of their effort on managing Antecedents. This means people are receiving little or no feedback (Consequences) when they do either right or wrong.

   Here's what we see all the time: If people aren't doing Vital Behaviors, most organizations make the mistake of doubling down on the Antecedents. Managers put up more posters in the break room ("Work Safely!") or send out emails reminding people what they need to do, but these Antecedents are about as effective as "Don't Park Here" signs!

   Why do managers focus on Antecedents when they don't work? First, because they are easy. And second, people don't understand how behavior really works—that it's driven by Consequences. Organizations that do get it spend most of their time catching people doing things right, and redirecting behaviors when they're not.

3. **5:1 feedback is the most powerful Consequence leaders have at their fingertips.** There is a proven Magic Feedback Ratio, which is 5:1 Positive to Constructive. A wonderful example comes from the world of marriage counseling. Drs. John and Julie Gottman spent 40+ years studying how married couples interact. Their simple research design required newly married couples to discuss a sore topic for 15 minutes. During that time, researchers tracked how many positive and negative behaviors each person displayed, including facial expressions (frowning, smiling), body language (arm crossing, leaning in) and verbal expressions. They then tracked those couples over many years to see if they stayed married.

Their results were astounding! When couples had a ratio of less than 5 positive interactions for each negative interaction (less than 5:1), it predicted divorce by year 5 with 87% accuracy! The 5:1 ratio was the bare minimum needed to stay in the marriage, and it became widely known as the Magic 5:1 Feedback Ratio (Figure 24).

THE MAGIC 5:1 FEEDBACK RATIO

Figure 24

Of course, businesses picked up on this concept and studied it. Even though some research has indicated the ratio is closer to 3:1 in business relationships, it's become very clear that people are more likely to stay in an organization when they get more positive feedback than constructive. We all appreciate being appreciated!

Chapter 14 Summary

- 50+ years ago Behavior Analysts pioneered a whole new area called Organizational Behavior Management (OBM) to create positive work environments that improve employee engagement and business results.

- The authors developed the Extended ABC Model to deal with the complexities of all the Antecedents and Consequences that can be delivered in organizations. They can be provided at two levels: (1) by the organization, and (2) within the work unit.

- To embed habits in an organization, you will need to align the A's and C's across both the organizational and work-unit levels, so they all work together to support Vital Behaviors.

- The most essential Antecedents are "Clear Expectations" and "Barrier Removal." The most critical Consequence is "Actionable Feedback." But employees might need other A's and C's beyond these three pillars to create lasting habits.

- Remember that Consequences are 4x more powerful than Antecedents in sustaining Vital Behaviors. Rewards make the behaviors worth doing again.

- If your organization has a problem with adherence or accountability, it's almost always a Consequence problem. Make sure you reinforce desired behaviors, and redirect undesired behaviors, rather than ignoring them.

- The Magic Feedback Ratio (5:1 Positive to Constructive) is the most powerful Consequence leaders have at their fingertips.

15

The Art of Navigating Emotions and Changing Mindsets

Sometimes, changing the external environment to support new habits isn't enough. It's also important to help individuals change their internal environment—their emotions and mindsets when they become stuck. *Lasting habits form only when a person's internal and external environments are aligned.* This means they do things they believe in and feel good about internally, and their external environment supports the Vital Behaviors. When this alignment occurs, the person has bought in and becomes more self-managed.

Throughout this book, you've learned that there is an objective science for identifying and embedding Vital Behaviors. But emotions and beliefs are more subjective—only the individual experiencing them can tell you what they are thinking and feeling. The art of behavior change involves understanding their thoughts and feelings to help them see if their internal and external environments are aligned. This chapter will help you gather information about emotions and mindsets and use it to help form new, lasting habits.

Deploying the Vital Behavior Blueprint Can Arouse Negative Feelings and Thoughts

"Maya" was a mid-level manager for a global manufacturer that was deploying a Vital Behavior Blueprint. It was going pretty well, but there were some problems that Maya will describe . . .

"We were in the middle of a challenging time at our company, facing a period of slow demand. Instead of just weathering the storm, our leadership saw an opportunity to enhance our performance, so we could come out stronger in the upturn. We all saw that we had gotten lax in our adherence to operational excellence.

"Our improvement approach was comprehensive. The objective? To transform every day into the perfect day for our operations across all our manufacturing sites. To achieve that, our leaders would need to do things very differently.

"We trained all 1,400 leaders, educating them on four Vital Behaviors they needed to start doing: (1) identify Vital Behaviors their direct reports needed to do consistently, (2) observe those behaviors frequently, (3) deliver both positive and constructive feedback to make those behaviors habits, and (4) eliminate barriers to success.

"We were committed to making Vital Behaviors work at all levels. Each leader received personalized coaching to implement a Vital Behavior Blueprint in their area. To gauge progress, we used quarterly surveys where direct reports rated their leaders' effectiveness in supporting their success.

"As a mid-level manager, I had a front-row seat to observe how different leaders adapted to the program. Initially, I was struck by the wide range of reactions. Some were upset about the imposition of new leadership requirements, while others clung to outdated beliefs like 'People don't need to be praised like dogs.'

"I quickly realized that it wasn't enough to focus solely on the Vital Behaviors and the external environment supporting them. For some people, we needed to address their emotional and mindset barriers to behavior change. Fortunately, we found a straightforward way to do that without having to become psychologists!"

3 Reactions to Change: RESILIENT, RECEPTIVE, or RESISTANT

Maya and other leaders at her company learned about three different ways people typically react to change: they can be Resilient, Receptive, or Resistant. It was very important for leaders to understand these reactions to change, because when change happens, it's essential to meet individuals where they are to help them implement Vital Behaviors.

Maya became adept at tailoring support to individuals based on their Resilience, Receptiveness, or Resistance to change. Personalizing support to each individual's unique needs was paramount to establishing buy-in. Here is how Maya adjusted her support strategies to assist each type of person effectively.

1. For RESILIENT people (about 15% of employees)

Maya watched some leaders get on Board immediately and quickly learn that the Vital Behaviors worked. These people achieved all pluses in Figure 25, meaning that these Resilient people were emotionally ready to make the change. Their mindset was good because they believed in the change. They actively aimed toward turning the new Vital Behaviors into lasting habits. And they found that those behaviors personally paid off and had a positive impact on their organization.

Resilient Reaction to Change

RESILIENT

This person has positive emotions and mindsets about the Vital Behaviors—and is turning them into habits that pay off personally and positively impact others.

Emotions	Mindsets	Vital Behaviors	Personal Payoffs	Impact on Others
+	+	+	+	+

Figure 25

Maya was grateful for the 15% of early adopters of Vital Behaviors:

"José was a great example of being Resilient. Following the leadership training, he immediately engaged his team to figure out the Vital Behaviors they needed to focus on. He even reached out to his coach within days of completing the training.

"My main challenge was keeping pace with him because he moved so swiftly. I held more frequent meetings with him in case he required assistance, but also to ensure he didn't get too far ahead of corporate milestones for the program!

"I thanked José for his exemplary role-modeling and asked him to share his success stories during morning huddles, as his colleagues held him in high regard. And when I asked if he would be open to coaching other leaders, he said sure, if approached.

"We were fortunate to have a small yet highly effective group of individuals like José. It gave us early momentum. Their success demonstrated to others that the new Vital Behaviors for leaders were effective."

Research by our colleague Dr. Laura Methot has shown that these early adopters achieve a 30% increase in all targeted performance indicators in their areas within four months—and maintain that edge over time. Below are some tips for supporting your people who are Resilient.

How Can Allies Assist Someone Who Is RESILIENT?

- Tell them how much you appreciate their willingness to try new things.

- Look for opportunities to catch them "doing things right."

- Show them how their Vital Behaviors contribute to targeted results.

- Thank them for being a role model.

- Ask them to tell you more about how they are turning Vital Behaviors into habits.

- Ask them to share their success stories at huddles and other meetings.

- Ask them if they are willing to coach others.

2. For RECEPTIVE people (about 70% of employees)

Most leaders in Maya's company saw the value in the new leadership behaviors. However, they found it challenging to do the behaviors consistently. As depicted in Figure 26, these people were Receptive to the change, generally having positive thoughts and feelings toward the Vital Behaviors.

What they struggled with was transforming their good intentions into lasting habits. Despite their efforts, they didn't see immediate benefits, especially during the initial stages of change when it felt particularly difficult. So, they became disheartened and considered giving up or doing only what was required.

Without the support of a coach or other Allies, these Receptive leaders would have reverted to their old habits of remaining in their offices instead of actively coaching employees on the manufacturing floor.

Receptive Reaction to Change

RECEPTIVE

This person has positive emotions and mindsets about the Vital Behaviors—but struggles to turn good intentions into habits that payoff for self and others.

Emotions	Mindsets	Vital Behaviors	Personal Payoffs	Impact on Others
+	+	−	−	−

Figure 26

Maya says the Receptive people were the 70% she spent the most time with.

"Such a huge percentage of our leadership was open to the change. At first, that felt great! When they came out of the leadership training session, they couldn't wait to get going. Yet I'd check back in a couple of weeks, and they had done little or nothing.

"I found that I had to check in at least weekly with these folks. They needed a lot of help to establish new habits. I spent time making sure they clearly understood the expectations. Many said they didn't have the time to do it, so I worked with them in large groups to reprioritize their tasks, even eliminating some completely.

"Their coaches helped them break down some of the Vital Behaviors into even tinier, more doable steps. For example, if they needed to meet with an employee to provide feedback, they started by just getting the meeting on the calendar.

"It was a lot of little and big things we did to embed these new Vital Behaviors as habits. We celebrated key milestones, like when everyone had identified mission-critical behaviors of employees in their work units, or when results improved. We connected leaders who were struggling with those leaders who were really good at the Vital Behaviors.

"Some leaders had been with us for decades, and they had learned to wait out any new initiative. But we were relentless in making sure everyone understood that these new leadership practices weren't going away. And we provided a steady stream of encouragement. We never let up. That's how they knew we were serious, so they kept working on it."

Dr. Methot's research showed that these Receptive people eventually caught up with their Resilient peers to produce remarkable results, but it took them an extra four months. Below are some tips for supporting people who are Receptive.

How Can Allies Assist Someone Who Is RECEPTIVE?

- Acknowledge that establishing new habits can be difficult, and it helps to seek encouragement early on.

- Help them explore ways to get encouraging support from other Allies, and offer to connect them.

- Check that they are clear about the expectations.

- Ask them to share their behavior change plans for the next few weeks—help them get specific.

- Help them break down Vital Behaviors into smaller steps, if needed.

- Help remove any barriers that are getting in their way.

- Provide specific, actionable feedback at least weekly, using the Magic Feedback Ratio of 5:1 Positive to Constructive feedback.

- Develop a plan to celebrate big and small achievements.

- Encourage them to recognize their own progress and provide self-feedback.

3. For RESISTANT people (about 15% of employees)

Some leaders resisted the change mightily. Some even threatened to quit unless the company relented! As illustrated in Figure 27, these Resistant people harbored primarily negative emotions toward the change and were unwilling to entertain other perspectives.

They either actively or passively resisted adopting new behaviors, hoping to simply wait it out. Because they weren't willing to give the Vital Behaviors a try, they never experienced the personal payoffs. Worse, their resistance discouraged others as they attempted to get people on their side and resist the change.

Resistant Reaction to Change

RESISTANT	Emotions	Mindsets	Vital Behaviors	Personal Payoffs	Impact on Others
This person has mainly negative thoughts and feelings about the Vital Behaviors—and is unwilling to try them, so they never experience the payoffs for self and others.	—	—	—	—	—

Figure 27

Maya says she had the hardest time with this 15% of employees. But she couldn't ignore their thoughts and feelings.

"I was taken aback by the level of anger some individuals displayed! For some of them, they were just stuck in their ways. They had been doing the same things for years and resisted trying new things. Other leaders dismissed the need employees had for positive recognition, believing the younger generation to be overly sensitive. They simply didn't want to be a part of it. I heard remarks like, 'Why should I have to thank people for showing up on time? What's wrong with these kids?'

"Initially, I found myself avoiding these Resistant individuals due to their negativity. When we did interact, I focused solely on the Vital Behaviors they needed to adopt, which only fueled their anger.

"I eventually realized the importance of understanding their thoughts and feelings about the change. I began acknowledging their concerns without judgment, and asked how I could support them in developing a more positive perspective. This approach revealed legitimate reasons behind their resistance.

"Some leaders believed people couldn't change, so we shared stories of successful behavior changes across all 22 sites. When some argued against the need for feedback, we solicited employee opinions on the matter.

"We were pleasantly surprised when front-line employees requested training on how to engage in two-way performance discussions. They even printed stickers for their helmets saying, 'Feedback is the breakfast of champions,' signaling their openness to feedback. It became clear they wanted to succeed too. Gradually, the Resistant leaders began to change, albeit very slowly.

"However, despite our efforts, about 5% of our leaders remained steadfastly Resistant. We provided a year for everyone to adjust their behaviors and offered ample support. Those who chose not to adapt were either moved out of leadership positions or offered exit packages. Failing to address their resistance would have jeopardized our credibility with the other 95% who eventually became exceptional leaders, propelling our company to the top of our industry."

Dr. Methot's research has shown that two-thirds of the 15% of Resistant leaders will eventually catch up to their Receptive and Resilient peers on all performance indicators—but it will take them three times as long to do so!

The other one-third (or a total of 5% of all leaders) will continue to resist and their work units will never catch up. That's when the organization needs to make some decisions about what to do with them.

How Can Allies Assist Someone Who Is RESISTANT?

- Acknowledge that change can be difficult and bring up many feelings.
- Ask how they are feeling about this change and reflect back their feelings without judging.
- Ask them to share their thoughts about the change and what they've experienced in the past with similar changes.
- Don't try to talk the person out of their negative thoughts. Instead:
  - Ask them what would make it work for them and remove any barriers.
  - Connect them with people internally and externally who have mastered the Vital Behaviors and can help them understand why they are important.
  - Help them understand the positive link between Vital Behaviors and targeted results.
  - Help them understand the impact on self and others if they choose not to do the Vital Behaviors.
- Once you've acknowledged their feelings and drawn out their thinking, encourage them to try the new Vital Behaviors. As they become Receptive to the change, switch to using those tips.

Help Everyone Become RESILIENT

To repeat, when an Ally Network is trying to embed new habits during a minor or major change, typically 15% of people will be Resilient, 70%

will be Receptive, and the remaining 15% will be Resistant. In these cases, the best thing Allies and leaders can do is create an external environment that supports 85% of people in trying new behaviors. Instead, many leaders fall into the trap of spending a lot of time and energy trying to change the internal environment of the 15% of people who are Resistant ("Why are they so angry?" or "I don't dare discuss that with them, it will upset them even more!"). This leaves 85% of people feeling unappreciated and ignored. Remember, the greatest advances can be made by spending the bulk of your time helping Resilient and Receptive people move forward.

For more substantial or emotionally taxing changes, such as reorganizations or business closures, the distribution may shift, with 15% displaying Resilience, 15% showing Receptiveness, and a whopping 70% exhibiting Resistance. In such scenarios, it can be immensely beneficial to spend time acknowledging an individual's thoughts and emotions before focusing on behavioral expectations. The tips we provided for assisting Resistant people offer a straightforward approach to understanding their internal landscape and determining the most effective means of support.

No matter if the changes your organization faces are large or small, it can be incredibly rewarding to help someone transition from Resistance to Resilience. Think back to the time you taught someone a new skill or helped them envision possibilities when they felt stuck. Or, perhaps you offered comfort and reassurance when they were feeling low, reminding them that tough times are temporary. Reflect on the sense of pride you experienced as they embraced new challenges and flourished.

We all encounter opportunities to make a difference in someone's life, whether through significant gestures or small acts of kindness. Choosing to lend a helping hand is one of the most fulfilling experiences imaginable, knowing that you've contributed to someone else's success!

Chapter 15 Summary

- There are three typical reactions to change: Resilient, Receptive, and Resistant.

- To develop lasting habits, the goal is to become Resilient so you are doing Vital Behaviors that you feel good about and believe in, and that pay off personally and have a positive impact on others.

- The 3 Reactions to Change model helps identify a person's current reaction to change and tips for helping them become Resilient. (See a summary of the tips on the next three pages.)

The 3 Reactions to Change

1. RESILIENT

This person has positive emotions and mindsets about the Vital Behaviors—and is turning them into habits that pay off personally and positively impact others.

Emotions	Mindsets	Vital Behaviors	Personal Payoffs	Impact on Others
+	+	+	+	+

How Can Allies Assist Someone Who Is RESILIENT?

- Tell them how much you appreciate their willingness to try new things.

- Look for opportunities to catch them doing things right.

- Show them how their Vital Behaviors contribute to targeted results.

- Thank them for being a role model.

- Ask them to tell you more about how they are turning Vital Behaviors into habits.

- Ask them to share their success stories at huddles and other meetings.

- Ask them if they are willing to coach others.

	Emotions	Mindsets	Vital Behaviors	Personal Payoffs	Impact on Others
2. RECEPTIVE This person has positive emotions and mindsets about the Vital Behaviors—but struggles to turn good intentions into habits that payoff for self and others.	+	+	−	−	−

How Can Allies Assist Someone Who Is RECEPTIVE?

- Acknowledge that establishing new habits can be difficult, and it helps to seek encouragement early on.

- Help them explore ways to get encouraging support from other Allies, and offer to connect them.

- Check that they are clear about the expectations.

- Ask them to share their behavior change plan for the next few weeks—help them get specific.

- Help them break down Vital Behaviors into smaller steps, if needed.

- Help remove any barriers that are getting in their way.

- Provide specific, actionable feedback using the Magic 5:1 Feedback Ratio of Positive to Constructive feedback.

- Develop a plan to celebrate big and small achievements.

- Encourage them to recognize their own progress and provide self-feedback.

3. RESISTANT	Emotions	Mindsets	Vital Behaviors	Personal Payoffs	Impact on Others
This person has mainly negative thoughts and feelings about the Vital Behaviors—and is unwilling to try them, so they never experience the payoffs for self and others.	—	—	—	—	—

How Can Allies Assist Someone Who Is RESISTANT?

- Acknowledge that change can be difficult and bring up many feelings.

- Ask how they are feeling about this change and reflect back their feelings without judging.

- Ask them to share their thoughts about the change and what they've experienced in the past with similar changes.

- Don't try to talk the person out of their negative thoughts. Instead:
  - Ask them what would make it all work for them and remove any barriers.
  - Connect them with people internally and externally who have mastered the Vital Behaviors and can help them understand why they are important.
  - Help them understand the positive link between Vital Behaviors and targeted results.
  - Help them understand the impact on self and others if they choose not to do the Vital Behaviors.

- Once you've acknowledged their feelings and drawn out their thinking, encourage them to try the new Vital Behaviors. As they become Receptive to the change, switch to using those tips.

In Conclusion, One More Promise to You . . .

At the beginning of this book, we made three promises to you. First, we promised to help you understand the crucial behaviors that drive success in your organization, work unit, or team. We hope the real-life stories we've shared have sparked ideas about which behaviors could make a real difference in your setting.

Perhaps you've already identified some obvious behaviors you can start working on immediately. Alternatively, you might need to conduct further research to pinpoint the 20% of behaviors that generate 80% of your desired outcomes. Once you've identified these Vital Behaviors that are tailored to your organization, focusing on them will simplify efforts, making it easier for everyone to help each other in achieving success day in and day out.

Second, we pledged to introduce a groundbreaking 5-Step method, the Vital Behavior Blueprint, for getting input and agreement from other stakeholders about which Vital Behaviors are most important. The Blueprint process will help you align and motivate people at scale, enabling them to support each other in executing Vital Behaviors. The Blueprint offers the quickest route to achieving this. We hope you've already begun the process with your team.

The third commitment we made is to teach you how to cultivate habits in a way that fosters daily appreciation for doing the right things. Our approach is designed to focus on the positive to produce not only outstanding results, but an engaged, satisfied workforce. Positive behavioral design features are purposefully built into the Vital Behavior Blueprint:

- Rooted in Behavior Analysis, the Blueprint emphasizes a non-blaming stance towards understanding why people behave as they do. Instead of blaming individuals, we examine the environment to identify factors influencing behavior.

- Our 5-Step method emphasizes high engagement by actively seeking and valuing employee opinions. Ally Networks eliminate the need for constant top-down management by connecting the right people to co-own Vital Behaviors and results every day.

- When Key Performers receive the 3 Pillars of clear expectations, actionable feedback, and barrier removal, they feel supported and listened to.

- The Magic Feedback Ratio (5:1 Positive to Constructive) underscores the importance of ensuring that actionable feedback leans more positive than negative. The result is that Allies acknowledge and reinforce Vital Behaviors more frequently than pointing out mistakes.

An Additional Promise You Wouldn't Have Believed Earlier

There's one more promise we didn't share at the beginning, because we believed you would require a deeper understanding of Ally Networks to fully embrace it. Our ultimate promise brings surprisingly good news: *Achieving organizational behavior change is easier than achieving individual behavior change.*

This is exemplified in the story shared at the beginning of Chapter 4 (rolling out a Corporate Health and Wellness program to remote workers). Who would have thought that a group of remote workers could unite to exercise, adopt healthier eating habits, and ultimately shed enough weight to improve the safety of their helicopter transportation to worksites? Such a transformation would have seemed impossible if attempted individually, but as a group . . .

There are powerful motivators already in place in organizations that make behavior change much easier for groups than for individuals:

- Employees recognize that organizations have the right to ask them to do things in a certain way, so Vital Behaviors add the clarity they need. For nonprofits, both volunteers and the people receiving services usually understand that the organization is asking them to do reasonable Vital Behaviors that will help them succeed.

- Most employees have lots of natural, personal motivation to do Vital Behaviors because they want to contribute, be appreciated, get a paycheck, keep their jobs, and progress professionally. For nonprofits, most people receiving services are personally motivated to keep receiving them. Volunteers also have personal motives for helping.

- Employees (and people receiving services from nonprofits) have ready access to a large network of Allies (leaders, peers, customers) who want them to succeed and are willing to provide social nudges and reinforcement.

Not only is organizational behavior change easier than individual behavior change: Ally Networks make any organizational performance improvement effort go more smoothly. Here are a few quotes from leaders around the globe who have used Ally Networks to execute their organizational plans:

"It's now exciting and fun for our people to adhere to repetitive safety and reliability practices—these are words I never thought would come out of my mouth!"

"Setting up our Ally Feedback Loops for the first time was like wiring an office IT network. Initially, it required careful planning to ensure the right people were connected. Later, we realized this same feedback network could support multiple Vital Behavior Blueprints simply by adding new "hubs" and "access points." Once the foundational infrastructure was in place, it became easier to achieve even more Behavior-Powered Results."

"Whenever we use this approach to execute a strategic initiative or big change, everything seems to work better."

"We get better alignment, accountability, and fluency in key business processes across our organization. Most importantly, our business unit now delivers predictable results and sustainable change."

"It was like Camelot. We could achieve anything we put our minds to."

Yes, large-scale behavior change within organizations is possible! We hope you now clearly understand Vital Behaviors and see how they supercharge any large-scale change effort with positive energy.

We can't wait to hear your own success stories!

MORE . . .

Want More Tools ?

Free templates that guide you through each step of building your own Vital Behavior Blueprint.

"The templates were a huge perk. I was immediately rewarded for completing a template because it helped me make sound decisions in building my overall Blueprint."

-Recent Workshop Participant

Get free gift now

https://members.vitalbehaviorblueprint.com/sign-up

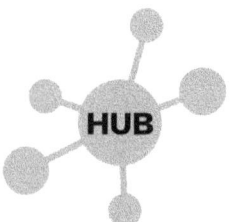

Behavior Blueprint HUB

Free Kickstart Resources

Get free resources such as the *Vital Behavior Blueprint Templates*, *Book Discussion Guide*, *Actionable Feedback* tips, and more!

Behavior Blueprint Builder Subscription

The Behavior Blueprint Builder is your all-in-one platform for building and managing your Vital Behavior Blueprints to execute any performance effort.

Features:
- Step-by-step video guides
- Interactive templates
- Automated pulse checks to:
  - Measure CORE Vital Behaviors for Leaders
  - Assess the strength of the 3 Pillars needed to build habits
- 3 Pillars Scorecard and barrier removal tracking system
- Blueprint Assist Center to get help from experts anytime

Join HUB now

https://members.vitalbehaviorblueprint.com/sign-up

Want to Learn More About Organizational Behavior Management (OBM)?

Behavior Analysis offers a comprehensive scientific framework that anyone can access. This framework includes core principles, terms, tools, scientific methods, and practical tools. If you want to become more knowledgeable in Behavior Analysis and its offshoot, Organizational Behavior Management, go to **www.obmnetwork.com** for resources you can turn to. Here you'll learn much more about how the ABC Model and the underlying laws of behavior have been applied successfully in organizations.

Acknowledgments

We stand on the shoulders of giants, and our journey in the world of Organizational Behavior Management (OBM) has been shaped by the wisdom and contributions of remarkable individuals and thinkers. Here, we thank them, as personally as we can . . .

First and foremost, B. F. Skinner, you have our profound gratitude as the visionary founder of Behavior Analysis. Your pioneering research laid the foundation for a more humanistic approach to understanding and addressing behavioral challenges. Instead of blaming individuals, you illuminated the transformative power of altering the external environment to foster success. Your groundbreaking work revealed the enduring Laws of Behavior, which continue to stand the test of time for individuals and organizations.

We extend our heartfelt thanks to the behavior analysts who expanded Skinner's insights to encompass the inner world of thoughts, beliefs, and emotions: Israel Goldiamond, Joe Layng, Steven C. Hayes, and others. Skinner always envisioned that these inner world events would someday be an integral part of a science-based analysis of behavior, and these dedicated researchers helped make that happen.

Our gratitude also goes to the authors who brought behavior change to the masses: James Clear, Charles Duhigg, and B. J. Fogg. Your popular books simplified decades of behavior analytic research, showing us the path for translating complex OBM strategies into our simplified 5-Step process for large-scale change.

In the early days of introducing Behavior Analysis to the business world, it was no small feat to convince organizations that behavior could be a root cause of poor performance. We thank the pioneers of OBM who created the core methodologies that illuminated the way for organizations to embrace this transformative approach. The giants in our field of OBM include Bill Abernathy, Leslie Braksick, Dale Brethower, Aubrey Daniels, Tom Gilbert, Dwight Harshbarger, Judi Komaki, Jon Krapfl, Tom Krause, Maria Malott, Richard Malott, Terry McSween, Bill Redmon, Geary Rummler, and Beth Sulzer-Azaroff. Your dedication and insights paved the path for OBM's adoption in top-tier organizations.

There are many other individuals and behavioral consulting firms currently elevating the application of OBM. We are deeply grateful to have connected with you as friends, colleagues, and learning partners over the years. You are incredibly willing to share your client experiences and expertise so we can all build this book of knowledge together.

We'd like to thank the following people for always being available at a moment's notice to discuss challenges in organizations and ways to advance our science: Carolina Aguilera, Beverly Begovich, Edward Blackman, Barbara Bucklin, Karen Bush, Phil Chase, Ivy Chong, John Dale, Alyce Dickinson, Paul Fjelsta, Patricia Floyd, E. Scott Geller, Shawn Gilroy, Ramona Houmanfar, Darnell Lattal, Joe Layng, Alan LeDuc, Patrick Marcotte, Heather McGee, Laura Methot, Kevin Munson, Mary Murray, Dottie Oakes, Hilary Potts, Mark Sasscer, Nika Simmons, Andressa Sleiman, Tom Spencer, Tracy Thurkow, and Warner Williams.

We are also deeply grateful for the invaluable contributions of our clients and colleagues from various disciplines who have helped us integrate OBM principles into traditional management systems:

- Dr. Jack Byrd and Jay (Julius) Stern, for creating the Center for Entrepreneurial Studies and Development, the pioneering consulting firm through which West Virginia University faculty and students transferred academic research in applied behavior analysis to improve performance in all types of business and industry across West Virginia and beyond. Jack, in particular, illuminated how systems engineering and throughput impact the selection of Vital Behaviors.

- Mark Sasscer and Connie Conboy, for integrating behavior change into national and international corporate quality management systems and change management practices.

- Jay Duffy, for establishing Behavior Analysis as the cornerstone of core leadership courses within a global company.

- Dr. Mikel Harry, co-founder of Six Sigma, and Warner Williams, a business unit leader, for collaborating on a simplified management framework focused on behavior-driven execution.

- David H. Freedman and Dr. Grant McCracken, for their efforts in modernizing and making the science of Behavior Analysis more accessible.

- Joe Jimenez and Gary Fischer, for their collaborative efforts in identifying the essential needs of CEOs and Project Leaders in executing global strategic initiatives.

We extend special gratitude to the many colleagues from the ALULA consultancy (formerly CLG) who spearheaded the development of methodologies that underpin our streamlined 5-Step approach. In particular, Leslie Braksick, a CLG co-founder, ensured the seamless integration of our work from the C-Suite to the frontline. Larry Lemasters, as a business executive and CLG co-founder, played a crucial role in recruiting numerous executives to the firm as consultants, ensuring a smooth alignment of OBM with traditional management systems. Steve Jacobs enriched our endeavors with invaluable organizational development insights. We are immensely grateful to the hundreds of colleagues at ALULA for their pioneering efforts in implementing OBM on an unprecedented scale. Many of the stories shared in this book are their stories, too, as well the stories of the clients they hold close in their hearts and minds.

We couldn't have made this book reach so many people without invaluable coaching from Steve Harrison, Becky Robinson, and their colleagues who we affectionately refer to as our "book doctors." Like trusted family doctors, they patiently listened to our questions and fears, and calmly guided us to the solution.

Special recognition goes to Fred Schroyer, Gretchen Kriesen, Lauren Howey, and Jim Scattaregia for their unparalleled editing and graphics support. It's been a true privilege to work with such talented professionals who are skilled at translating scientific concepts into engaging content. Thank you!

Finally, we express our deepest gratitude to our amazing spouses, Mickey Heston and Tim Ludwig. You have provided unwavering support in all our endeavors. Your understanding of the impact our science can have on the world is invaluable, and we are fortunate to have you by our sides in pursuing this cause.

Together, these incredible individuals have shaped our journey and empowered us to share the transformative power of OBM with the world.

With heartfelt thanks,

Julie and Lori

About The Authors

Dr. Julie Smith is a trailblazer in large-scale organizational behavior change, with a knack for achieving mission impossible. As a co-founder of ALULA, a premiere behavior-based strategy execution firm, her methodologies, backed by decades of successful case studies with top-tier clients, have earned global acclaim. She then founded Performance Ally after family members experienced life-changing healthcare events caused by human error. Recognizing the difficulty of establishing even the simplest behaviors as habits, especially in healthcare settings, Performance Ally developed a "pocket coach" that provides the same personalized behavior-change guidance offered by seasoned organizational behavior consultants. Their enterprise application, Ally Assist™, simplifies the behavior-change journey, making the science of organizational habit formation accessible to all companies, large or small.

Dr. Lori Ludwig is renowned for her extraordinary skill in guiding organizations to align strategy with processes, roles, and behaviors, resulting in high-impact, meaningful results. With 20+ years of consulting experience across diverse sectors, ranging from Fortune 500s to nonprofits and small businesses, Lori's work has had a transformative impact on a global scale. Her projects—from pioneering performance-based learning strategies to fostering collaborations around shared goals—have elevated productivity and delivered tremendous value for her clients. Serving as Chief Performance Architect at Performance Ally, her mission is to disseminate the science of Organizational Behavior Management (OBM) to create large-scale positive change. Lori simplifies its application, empowering organizations to unleash human potential, amplify impact, and navigate complexity effectively.

Author Contacts:

- Dr. Julie M. Smith and Dr. Lori Ludwig
- PERFORMANCE ALLY
- **jsmith@performanceally.com**
- **lludwig@performanceally.com**

About Performance Ally

Performance Ally™ is revolutionizing how organizations align and motivate people to build habits at scale. If you struggle to turn even the simplest behaviors into habits in your organization, we can help. Our groundbreaking, user-friendly tools enable you to identify and implement mission-critical Vital Behaviors leading to a quantum improvement in business results:

- **Vital Behavior Blueprint**™—our pioneering 5-Step formula for aligning Vital Behaviors with your organizational goals and fostering an environment where Allies support each other to convert Vital Behaviors into enduring habits.

- **Ally Assist**™—our flagship enterprise application connects leaders, associates, and customers in realtime. They help each other clarify expectations, give immediate feedback, and remove barriers to ensure Vital Behaviors become embedded as cultural habits.

Our tools replicate and surpass the personalized guidance of costly organizational behavior consultants. Our definitive guide, *Vital Behavior Blueprint: 5 Steps to Embed Mission-Critical Habits into Your Organization's DNA*, plus interactive online templates, self-guided workshops, expert advisory support, and certification programs, will motivate your entire team to master our tools and attain individual and collective success. You can learn more at **www.performanceally.com**.

Notes

These notes are keyed to page numbers in each chapter.

OUR DISCOVERY OF THE ART AND SCIENCE OF VITAL BEHAVIORS

3   **Healthcare professionals typically adhered to best practices less than 40% of the time:**

1. Ament, S.M., de Groot, J.J., Maessen, J.M., Dirksen, C.D., van der Weijden, T., & Kleijnen, J. "Sustainability of professionals' adherence to clinical practice guidelines in medical care: a systematic review." *BMJ Open,* December 29, 2015.

2. Amorin-Woods, L.G., Beck, R.W., Parkin-Smith, G.F., Lougheed, J., & Bremner, A.P. (2014). "Adherence to clinical practice guidelines among three primary contact professions: A best evidence synthesis of the literature for the management of acute and subacute low back pain." *The Journal of the Canadian Chiropractic Association*, 58(3), 220–237. www.ncbi.nlm.nih.gov/pmc/articles/PMC4139767

Chapter 1

14   **It's been estimated that over 50% of needed performance improvement efforts fail:** Kotter, John. *Leading Change.* Boston: Harvard Business Review Press, 2012.

14   **It takes 17 years on average to get new, life-saving procedures to be adopted:** Morris Z.S., Wooding S., & Grant, J. "The answer is 17 years, what is the question: Understanding time lags in translational research." *Journal of the Royal Society of Medicine* 104(12):510–20 (December, 2011).

15	**The 80/20 rule was discovered by economist Vilfredo Pareto:** Wikipedia, accessed 1 May 2024: https://en.wikipedia.org/wiki/Joseph_M._Juran.
15	**In 1941, quality expert Joseph M. Juran found that the 80/20 rule was a universal principle, applicable to a wide range of situations beyond economics, and was especially helpful in explaining quality issues:** Lean Enterprise Institute, 2024: www.lean.org/lexicon-terms/pareto-chart
15	**Richard Koch's seminal book, *The 80/20 Principle: Achieve More with Less*, extended the application of the 80/20 Rule beyond business to help millions of people succeed in personal life:** Koch, R. *The 80/20 Principle: Achieve More with Less*. Boston, MA: Nicholas Brealey Publishing, 2022.
16	**When customers have a single, terrible customer experience, 67% of them will take their business elsewhere:** Esteban Kolsky, 2015, www.slideshare.net/ekolsky/cx-for-executives#2.
17	**In healthcare, Dr. Peter Pronovost developed and tested a 5-Step checklist for preventing central line catheter infections:** Pronovost, P. & Vohr, E. *Safe Patients, Smart Hospitals: How One Doctor's Checklist Can Help Us Change Health Care from the Inside Out*. New York, NY: Hudson Street Press; 2010.
17	**Employees crave recognition and appreciation—a seemingly small thing. When they don't get it, every major business result suffers—quality, productivity, engagement, retention**: Quantum, 2023: www.quantumworkplace.com/future-of-work/importance-of-employee-recognition
17	**Vital Behavior: Handwashing by healthcare workers. Care providers wash their hands at the right times only about 30% of the time:** Sickbert-Bennett E.E., DiBiase, L.M., Willis, T.M., Wolak, E.S., Weber, D.J., & Rutala, W.A. "Reduction of Healthcare-Associated Infections by Exceeding High Compliance with Hand Hygiene Practices." *Emerging Infectious Diseases*, 22(9):1628–30 (September 22, 2016).
17	**If 100% of healthcare workers followed handwashing procedures, roughly 1 million lives would be saved each year in just the United States:** Curtis, V. & Camicross, S. "Effect of washing hands with soap on diarrhoea risk in the community: A systematic review." *Lancet Infectious Diseases*, 2003, 3(5):275–81.
18	**Vital Behaviors: Eating roots and talking about food:** From a case study used by ALULA to train internal and external consultants. Original source unknown.

19	**Here are a few situations our clients and colleagues faced where Vital Behaviors dramatically improved the outcomes**: Quotes are from our client case studies and three successful business books written by ALULA, a premier behavior-based strategy execution consultancy co-founded by the lead author of this book.
20	**Surgical complications fell by 36%. Deaths decreased substantially by 47%:** Gawande, Atul. *The Checklist Manifesto*. London: Profile Books, 2011.

Chapter 2

29	**Dr. Rackham observed 35,000 sales calls across 27 countries to identify the Vital Behaviors:** Rackham, Neil. *SPIN Selling*. New York: McGraw-Hill Education, 1988.
32	**Several of our colleagues have continued to develop what our clients originally christened "Behavioral Lean Six Sigma."** In the first two decades of the 2000s, the Continuous Learning Group (now ALULA, www.alula.clg.com) developed this next-generation technology by integrating Applied Behavior Science into Lean Sigma, based on work done by Paul Fjelsta (www.linkedin.com/in/paulfjelsta).
33	**Another striking example of cornerstone behaviors comes from a project we had with a vast national railroad:** Johnson, J., Dakens, L., Edwards, P. and Morse, N. *SwitchPoints: Culture Change on the Fast Track to Business Success*. New York: John Wiley & Sons, 2008.
34	**One healthcare consulting firm identified mission-critical behaviors that it said reliably improved patient satisfaction ratings:** Studer, Q. *Results That Last: Hardwiring Behaviors That Will Take Your Company to the Top*. New York: Wiley, 2007.
35	**Even Quint Studer, the creator of these behaviors, has changed his approach. In his new book, *Rewiring Hardwiring*, he now advocates for letting healthcare workers customize Vital Behaviors:** Studer, Q. and Collard, D. *Rewiring to Excellence: Hardwired to Rewired*. Gratitude Group Publishing, 2024.

Chapter 3

38	**Only 21% of U.S. workers strongly agree their performance is managed in a way that motivates them to do outstanding work:** Gallup, *State of the American Workplace report*, 2020.
39	**Research by Gallup shows that only 30% of U.S. workers get all 3 Pillars:** Gallup, *State of the American Workplace report*, 2020.

39 **When Gallup correlated its survey results with actual organizational performance, they found that when 80% of workers received this essential performance support, numerous performance indicators dramatically improved:** Gallup, *State of the American Workplace report*, 2020. Gallup's findings on performance improvement data are supported by decades of research published in the *Journal of Organizational Behavior Management (JOBM)*. The findings are further supported by client case studies from ALULA, a premier behavior-based strategy execution consultancy, co-founded by the lead author of this book.

40 **A colleague of ours, Dr. Laura Methot, conducted extensive research to identify the crucial turning point that signals when an individual has successfully transformed Vital Behaviors into reliable habits:** Unpublished research conducted in 2014.

47 **In 2019, across their 182 sites, a remarkable 73% managed to achieve zero injuries:** www.dupont.com/about/sustainability/deliver-world-class-health-safety-performance.html.html

48 **Our colleague, Dr. Judith Komaki, has spent her life researching the behaviors of leaders who produce extraordinary results like DuPont has:** Komaki, Judith L. *Leadership from an Operant Perspective*. London: Routledge, 1998.

Chapter 6

75 **Occasionally we've been asked to quantify how behavioral consistency will improve a targeted result. When that is needed, we use the conceptual measure called the Potential for Improving Performance (PIP) developed by Thomas F. Gilbert, a pioneer in Human Performance Engineering:** Gilbert, T. F. *Human Competence: Engineering Worthy Performance (Tribute edition)*. San Francisco, CA: Pfeiffer, 2007.

78 **Research shows that only 10–20% of the knowledge gained in training is put into practice at work.** U.S. Office of Personnel Management (OPM), Training Transfer—Training and Development Policy Wiki, Helpful Tips. www.opm.gov/wiki/training/Training-Transfer/Print.aspx#:~:text=Research%20indicates%20that%20only%20about,is%20transferred%20into%20the%20workplace

Chapter 8

100 **Yet there is a reason why, as the American Society of Anesthesiologists reports, about a dozen sponges and other surgical instruments are left inside patients' bodies every day, resulting in 4,500–6,000 cases per year in the US:** CNN Health, "Surgical sponges left inside woman for at least 6 years," February 21, 2018, www.cnn.com/2018/02/21/health/surgical-sponges-left-inside-woman-study/index.html.

Chapter 9

109 **A remarkable example of Ally Feedback Loops in action comes from Iceland:** www.independent.co.uk/life-style/health-and-families/iceland-knows-how-to-stop-teen-substance-abuse-but-the-rest-of-the-world-isn-t-listening-a7526316.html

113 **Survey completion rates are typically below 20%:** www.genroe.com/blog/acceptable-survey-response-rate-2/11504

Chapter 11

130 **NPS® is a well-known measure of customer loyalty:** Reichheld, F.F. *The Loyalty Effect*. Boston: Harvard Business School Press, 2001.

Chapter 13

174 **Behavior Analysis provides the way for organizations to "drive out fear," which is one of the "14 Points for Management" developed by business management guru Dr. W. Edward Deming:** Deming, W.E., Orsini, J., & Cahill, D.D. *The Essential Deming: Leadership Principles from the Father of Quality*. New York: McGraw Hill, 2012.

174 **If you are seeking a simple way to get started, these best-selling books… provide practical ways for individuals to break old habits and make new ones:** Clear, James. *Atomic Habits: Tiny Changes, Remarkable Results: An Easy & Proven Way to Build Good Habits & Break Bad Ones*. New York: Avery, an imprint of Penguin Random House, 2018.

Duhigg, Charles. *The Power of Habit: Why We Do What We Do in Life and Business*. New York: Random House, 2014.

Fogg, B.J. *Tiny Habits: The Small Changes that Change Everything*. Boston: Houghton Mifflin Harcourt, 2019.

177 **No wonder 80% of New Year's resolutions are forgotten by February:** www.driveresearch.com/market-research-company-blog/new-years-resolutions-statistics/#:~:text=Just%209%25%20of%2adults%20keep,first%20week%20of%20the%20year.

179 **But over the last three decades, Behavior Analysis has evolved new models to help understand how our internal world of emotions, thoughts, and beliefs are shaped by the external environment and affect our behaviors:** Essential components of the new models include:

Acceptance and Commitment Therapy (ACT)—helps people break through negative thoughts and emotions by being mindful of them and accepting them as part of life, rather than having them become drivers of poor behaviors.

Relational Frame Theory (RFT)—explains how people learn complex relationships among words, ideas, and events; gets to the heart of how perceptions and beliefs form and how to change them.

Nonlinear Contingency Analysis—helps people understand "disturbing" behavioral, emotional, and thought patterns and the complex relationships between multiple cues and rewards that maintain those patterns. The goal is to analyze what rewards the person gets for these disturbing patterns and how to get the same rewards for more productive behaviors.

Chapter 14

181 **OBM is the study and application of Behavior Analysis in organizations:** See www.obmnetwork.com.

186 **The Magic Feedback Ratio (5:1 Positive to Constructive) is the most powerful Consequence leaders have at their fingertips:** J.M. Gottman and J.S. Gottman. *The Science of Couples and Family Therapy: Behind the Scenes at the Love Lab.* New York: W.W. Norton, 2018, p. 340.

www.ingramcontent.com/pod-product-compliance
Lightning Source LLC
Chambersburg PA
CBHW052128030426
42337CB00028B/5070